DONNCHA

WALKING AND TALKING

WITH

DONNCHA O DULAING

Best wishes,

Donncha Ó Dúlaing

BLACKWATER PRESS

Editor
Aidan Culhane

Design & Layout
Paula Byrne

Cover Design
Liz Murphy

ISBN
0 86121 955 4

© – 1998 Donncha O Dulaing

Produced in Ireland by
Blackwater Press
c/o Folens Publishers
8 Broomhill Business Park,
Tallaght, Dublin 24.

Contents

Beginnings 1

The Best of Times 13

Ballyshane and The Summer of Boyhood 34

My University Days .41

The Years Of Our Ford 55

RTE – The Cork Story 62

Brave New Flawed World 74

Highways and Byways 84

Christy Ring: The Cuchulainn of Cloyne 97

Footsteps Into Time – Beginnings 105

Marathon Monday 1984 110

The Longest Walk of All!
    Donncha's Ireland Walk 115

The Promised Land .121

Images of Jerusalem .127

In The Steps of O'Sullivan Beara 143

Farewell and Fáilte 155

Beginnings

Doneraile, Co. Cork was as good a place as anywhere to be born and there I appeared in the world on 15 March 1933, arriving weak and long before I was expected. I was quickly baptised Denis Patrick Dowling in St Mary's Parish Church. Sister Kevin, a local Presentation Sister, gave my mother a small bottle of Lourdes water 'to help the poor baby'. Our nearest neighbours in Convent Road, an adjunct of Taypot Lane, looked on admiringly as my mother wheeled me out into the late spring sunshine. Taypot Lane was so called because of a local propensity for throwing tea leaves out front doors to flow away down the little shores in a timid brown trickle of lukewarm water.

My father, Daniel Dowling, was a Kerryman from Glenmore, near Camp on the Dingle peninsula, although I never heard him talk of it, nor indeed do I ever remember him going back to his Dingle Peninsula roots. It would be more than sixty years later before the reality of my Kerry patrimony would be introduced to me by my cousin, Denis from Springfield, Massachusetts. He was to bring with him letters, photographs and stories of my father's distant past. The Kerry 'connection' would live again. I heard later, however, that hardly a week went by without my father sending a plug of tobacco to his mother, an avid pipe smoker. My mother, whose maiden name was Helena Cashman, came from East Cork – Ballyshane in the parish of Aghada where I spent many of the happiest summers of my boyhood and youth during and after the Second World War. My father used to say that I was the product of a mixed marriage, he was from Kerry and my mother from Cork. Thankfully it never seriously affected my love for either county, the kingdom of football and the rebel county in hurling.

I was the eldest. My two sisters, Mary and Kitty, were also born in the little house on Convent Road in Doneraile. 'Granny', not my real grandmother but a kindly old lady, who helped my mother with my two sisters and myself was my introduction to folklore. Her stories were real and gothic. She told of coaches hurtling blindly up the avenue and out the back gate of Doneraile Court with some headless St Leger landlord presiding over a wild frenzy of ghostly horror.

We learned of the lord who was bitten by his tame fox and who died roaring because they had 'to smother the old ruffian between two ticks'. The cause of his death may have been more prosaic. He was most probably 'put down', or smothered between heavy bedclothes because there was no cure for his syphilitic complaint. By the way, the marks of that fox's chain are still to be seen on the wall at Doneraile Court. 'Granny' always had a moral to her tales. She said that the fox also bit the coachman who survived because he wore leather gloves but the lords always wore silk.

Arthur Young, the nineteenth century traveller and historian, described Doneraile as 'a neat village' although J. Crofton Croker in his *Researches in the South of Ireland* was somewhat less than complimentary: 'This was the only occasion on which we met with difficulty in seeing any gentleman's grounds. After exploring the unpicturesque and miserable town we returned to our dirty inn.' He is, however, contradicted once again by Arthur Young, 'The country within two or three miles of Doneraile, ranks among the best I have seen in Ireland; it is varied, much improved, well wooded and very cheerful.'

Doneraile Court, home of the St Legers, was a mysterious place in my childhood. Elizabeth St Leger, the lady freemason as famous as the mad, sexually energetic Hayes St Leger, lives on with great affection in local folklore. We're told that on one occasion she hid herself in an alcove to eavesdrop on a freemasons' meeting and was only discovered when the clock struck twelve. Lord Doneraile was most upset and, within minutes, she was made a mason. We were also told that a certain gentleman with a cloven hoof often attended the weekly meetings. He, unlike Elizabeth, was never discovered, and so never joined the masons.

Sometime in the mid-1960s I visited the last Lady Doneraile at the Court and then, later when she was dead and the Court abandoned, I presented an edition of 'My Own Place' on RTE television from these scenes of my childhood.

The Court, although empty, seemed to hint at other times, perhaps the vaguest scent, the most imaginary rustle of a shawl, brittle tinkle of ghostly laughter as the St Legers and their friends climbed the staircase to look out wide windows across untroubled Augustan landscapes when no Doneraile conspiracies ever invaded the privileged quiet of Anglo-Ireland and no hint of future desolation clouded the skies.

Lady Doneraile, gone like all the rest, scurried across my memory, reminding me that Sir Philip Sidney, Elizabethan and adventurer had once loved the lime walks that Sir Walter Raleigh, pipe-smoking and potato-proposing once visited and that the demesne had been once the property of Edmund Spenser who wrote 'The Faerie Queen' not five miles away and whose son was shaved to bloody death by his irate wife in Mallow – she slit his throat. Spenser might have been prophetic as well as poetic:

> The mirrhe sweete bleeding in the bitter wound,
>
> the Warlike beech, the Ash for nothing ill.

Our garden ended at the demesne wall and my earliest morning memories are of pigeons calling out their peaceful anthem, 'Buy two cows Davy, buy two cows Davy'. These were, I am sure, cousins to the birds who lived near the Catholic and Protestant churches, ecumenical in monotony of call and location. The Protestant church, where lie generations of the quiet dead, was where I found the motto of the St Legers, 'Haut et Bon' – high and good. They lie under the ground that they couldn't get enough of in life and, now, cannot get out of, in death.

Here lies Lady Castletown who must have loved peaches, apples and grapes. Her simple lord husband fed her posthumous habit night after night, putting fruit on the grave, while the local youngsters ensured her perpetual hunger, spending happy mornings gorging themselves with the same St Leger fruit.

It was at Doneraile Steeple that the first steeplechase ended. It began from Buttevant Steeple and ended at ours. From this began the Aintree Grand National and every steeplechase that followed. The St Legers too, had a great race named after them, and later we re-created our steeplechase for television. I have happy memories of Tim Donovan and other intrepid horsemen setting out on the hazardous journey.

The Awbeg River, a tributary of the lovely Blackwater, flowed near the Protestant Church and often on summer days we watched bleating sheep protestingly dipped in a Jeyes-fluid smelling solution which, if we stood too close, often flecked our collops with an exquisite icy shock. The collops, 'colpaí' in Irish, are that part of the leg from the back of the knee to the foot! Before I leave the Protestant church I must remember the bells and the bell ringers, among them Billy Evans from Carker and all those who rang out the old and the new during the turning years of childhood.

Talking of Protestants, I remember Alfie Buckley and other school pals who ate their sandwiches, drank their milk and enjoyed the sun while, we unwilling and irate, studied Catechism and religious instruction – we envied them, although they had their instructions in Sunday School!

Lord Doneraile was our landlord. He was the owner of many houses in the village, I never saw him in my childhood, but Hamilton, his agent. was well-known. It was to him we paid the rent. I often delivered this to the estate office across the river from the Christian Brothers school. Hamilton sat behind his desk and generally took the few shillings without a word or a smile. Sometimes, he gave me a penny for myself, with which I would buy a penny ice-cream at Titridge's Shop where I also in later times bought the *Dandy* and the *Beano*. One day, however, he smirked and said, 'Ah young Dowling, Mickey Rooney pays your rent'! He referred to my mother's beads bag in which she sent the rent. It was a little black bag bearing the legend 'MR' for 'My Rosary' on the flap. His unsubtle sectarian quip, so unlike the attitudes of our other Protestant neighbours and friends, stung even a small boy and has remained with me since. He was a perfect example of his type.

* * *

What can I say of my first day at school? Not much. I ran home to Mother only to be rapidly returned to the nuns by a very irate father. My thoughts go back to Sr Gerard, Sr Columba, Sr Anna, Sr Colman and Mother Benignus. They were all gentle women who gave their time and their lives to caring.

Going and coming from school were cherished adventures. In May we looked forward to lessons in the Convent Garden, where at an outside May altar, fresh flowers and 'I'll sing a hymn to Mary' rose to the blue heavens in an anthem to the Virgin. Sometimes I shared an egg with Miss O'Connell, and got to look at her niece who was attending the secondary school. I fell in love, silently of course. She was my first love and I never saw her again.

Those warm days of wartime summers are always with me. The nuns, alas, almost all gone now, have never aged. The convent chapel, dark and mysteriously wax-smelling, the songs of blackbirds and thrushes and the gentle slope down to the swan-filled Awbeg River are immutable testaments to childhood.

Miss Lee, a small mysterious woman, was a next door neighbour when we lived in the New Road where we moved in the early 1940s. She had an orchard and often stored her freshly picked apples in chamber pots. I never ate even one! She had a small flock of bantam hens and a cock who endangered his life by crowing in the early mornings disturbing all the neighbours. I remember having my ear clipped by my father when an older, wiser boy told me to run in with the news that 'Miss Lee's cock is riding all the hens!' Sometimes it does not pay to tell the truth.

Schooling continued, a blur of tables, marla, tears, sandwiches, lukewarm milk and a rattling of nuns' beads, rushing home like an Awbeg trout, and learning for the first time that Sunday noon will come too soon and so will Monday morning!

Sad to say, an old lady wrote to *Fáilte Isteach* to tell me that all the dear nuns have been dug up and moved to another place, their peace in the old convent graveyard savagely disturbed, taken away from the sound of convent bell and the smell of convent chalk to make way for buyers of the empty convent. All the memories of Canon Sheehan's visits to the convent whipped away and no one could do anything. Is this progress – God help us!

I left 'high infants' in the Presentation Convent and entered the wider world of the Christian Brothers National School, and who could forget the Christian Brothers? The little school was down by the river, where Brother McInerney, Brother O'Donohue, Michael Riordan and a young man called Brother Magee taught us our lessons. Incidentally Brother Magee is alive and well like myself and now living in Dun Laoghaire and he and I share many a night and the odd libation as we remember the classes of long ago – the Hunters, the Phelans, the Goulds, the Slatterys, the Lenehans, the Walshes and many others who shared those early days of primary education with us. I am glad to say that Brother Magee's memories are as sunny as my own and we hope to go on talking and libating for a good while yet.

These times of my young boyhood in Doneraile remind me of the blackout. I see again the fishman on Fridays shouting 'fresh hers, fresh hers' (herring). I hear the tiny wireless in the morning while my father whistled as he shaved near the small mirror in the back kitchen. I recall my red-haired mother singing to us by the fire on wintry evenings, teaching me my first song: 'The Minstrel Boy' and reciting O'Kelly's epic 'The Curse of Doneraile', and its crawthumping sequel, 'The Blessing of Doneraile'.

O'Kelly was of Clare extraction and most likely a travelling poet, whose much prized watch was 'lost' in Doneraile. He remembered:

Alas! how dismal is my tale

I lost my watch in Doneraile

My Dublin watch, my chain and seal

Pilfer'd at once in Doneraile.

May beef, or mutton, lamb or veal

Be never found in Doneraile;

> May heav'n a chosen curse entail
> On rigid, rotten Doneraile.
> Oh! may my couplets never fail
> To find new curse in Doneraile.

He went on in this vituperative vein for quite a long time until the Lady Doneraile of the time presented him with a replacement timepiece. He was pleased to write:

> How vastly pleasing is my tale,
> I found my watch in Doneraile.
> My Dublin watch, my chain and seal
> Were all restored at Doneraile.
> May beef and mutton, lamb and veal
> Plenty create at Doneraile.
> May heav'n each chosen bliss entail
> On honest, friendly Doneraile;
> And may its Lady never fail
> To find new joys in Doneraile.

Incidentally, O'Kelly is reported to have met King George IV during a visit to Dublin; the King in a rare moment of sobriety, observed, 'I see Mr. O'Kelly, like your two great contemporaries, Scott and Byron, you are lame.' Undaunted, our Doneraile Bard replied:

> Three poets of three different nations born
> The United Kingdom at this age adorn –
> Byron of England, Scott of Scotia's blood,
> And Erin's pride, O'Kelly, great and good.

Sound Man!

* * *

There were always hurling matches in the 'horse close' (a horse paddock belonging to the St Legers) that reminded one of Canon Sheehan's novel, *Glenanaar*, where the spirit of north Cork is stirred in an opening passage:

> Not a word broke from that whirling mass as the heavy ball rolled swiftly over the level grass as some young athlete, with the fleetness of a deer, tapped it on before him, until he brought it within reach of the coveted goal. You heard only the patter of feet, the light or heavy tap tap tap on the ball, the crack of the camáns as they cross in the air above or on the grass beneath; and now and again the screams of women or girls, who

stampeded wildly when the ball was driven into their midst, and the fierce flying combatants, with their heaving breasts and staring eyes, forgot their chivalry and carried the tumult of battle right in amongst their excited sisters.

Canon PA Sheehan, the novelist and essayist, whose novels *Glenanaar* and *My New Curate* were favourites, not just in Ireland, but in mainland Europe as well, lived in Doneraile from 1895 until his untimely death in 1913. Often on my way to serve early Mass in the parish church I would stop at his grave and admire the plastic angels and wonder what the tomb inscriptions meant. He was much loved and during his last illness the road outside his house was covered in straw to muffle the steel ring of creamery cart wheels on their morning journey. The late John Walshe of Laharn was his friend and admirer and once remarked to me, 'they said that he was a proud man but he was never that. He was gentle, kind and considerate and a great man to preach a sermon'.

I served early Mass for one of his successors, Canon Maurice O'Connell and was often invited into the Canon's house and whenever I visited his garden I often sat in Canon Sheehan's garden seat, perhaps inviting literary inspiration. Indeed, another old friend, Mrs Shine, told me that he loved flowers, all except for those coloured yellow. He detested yellow. It reminded him of convict garb during his days as a chaplain in Dartmoor.

I often served Mass for Fr Andrew Barry in the sanatorium in Heatherside. Here, wraithlike creatures froze in the out of doors as the unfortunate sufferers from consumption or TB strove to survive the most rampant curse in Ireland. One morning after the tea-and-boiled-egg breakfast of Heatherside, Fr Andrew, who was a very nice man, asked me how long I had been left-handed. I said that I wasn't and he asked why then did I always hold my tea-cup in my left hand. I replied that my mother told me to do this because the patients probably drank with the cup in their right hand and so I would avoid taking consumption. The priest laughed all the way home and gave me a ten shilling note for myself.

Mrs Kearney was the local chapel woman and often on my way home from school I would call into the church to see her dusting and to help her remove candlewax from the altar. One evening at dusk, she asked me to go to the end of the church to light the candles around a coffin which I did with shaking hand as I expected Mr Murphy, who lay inside, to sit up and say something – which he didn't. It made me realise that chapel man was another career not open to me.

The missions were very important in our lives. All the parish, most of them anyway, attended and on the long summer evenings we rode the bicycles of the penitents up and down the main street until the bell rang out at the elevation of the host during benediction, summoning all sinners to prayer. We always stopped and looked up and down the main street but we never saw anyone coming. I suppose all the sinners must have been inside.

One day, I was sent to the end of the garden with jam sandwiches and a bottle of milk and told to stay quiet. About an hour later Nurse Herlihy came down and told me I had a lovely baby sister. I was delighted until I saw her. She couldn't talk, only screamed with a very red little face and wrinkled hands and her name was Kitty. She could only improve after that – and she did.

We moved house in the early 1940s and I recall the installation of the electric light, which Granny called 'the light of heaven', a light which filled all our corners and banished away forever little spirits of times past.

The Pictures of course came to Doneraile and not without controversy. Mr McDonald of McDonalds Amusements built a cinema on a site near the Catholic church which did not please the parish priest. He spoke about it off the pulpit suggesting that sex would jump rampant off the screen into the lives of all the innocent people of Doneraile, forgetting that the St Legers had spread sex far and wide long before this. Anyway, to make a long story short, Mr McDonald, who was a Presbyterian but who sent all his children to the local Catholic schools, was hurt but not to be deflected. Black and white movies came to Doneraile and we saw people whom we had never seen before, close up and moving and even talking. James Cagney, Bing Crosby, Bob Hope, Dorothy Lamour and others became our forever friends and the Canon conveniently forgot about sin and we all lived more or less happily ever afterwards.

My father, who was a great whistler, was as fond of circuses as I was and often brought me on his bicycle to Buttevant to Duffys' Circus where I once saw a performer sing 'Beautiful Dreamer' and realised for the first time that one day, I must surely be a star of the silver screen. This reminds me that I once entered a talent contest in Doneraile and scandalised my cousin who was minding me when I rushed up onto the stage, uninvited and rendered twice an unlikely version of 'Baa Baa Blacksheep'. As I was then six years of age, I didn't win the contest and they will never know what they missed.

During the war, the older men would gather at the cross in the evenings to discuss the advances or the retreats of the allies or the Nazis. They were, by the way, mostly pro-German and listened avidly to Lord Haw Haw. One evening there was a row and I heard for the first time what my mother called 'the soldiers' word'. One man addressed another as 'the fucking seed of a black and tan'. I ran in of course to tell my father what I heard and his reply was 'never let me hear that in our house again' which he didn't.

* * *

We were, I suppose, a society poised between Anglo and Irish, drawing the best from both and entirely happy with both. As I look back now I find it difficult to find anything that dissatisfied me except having to go to school. I remember lovely summer evenings picking flowers, bluebells in the quarry, catching bees, bumblers and red asses, bowling hoops, helping to milk cows and eating tons of sandwiches that my father made in the kitchen and put on a plate on the window outside the front door for all and sundry to partake of. After all that there were the long, long dusks of boyhood as the sun went down and the moon came up over the demesne wall and the owls sang their song of night and the bats, much feared, surged in around the lights and it was time for bed and the end of just another day in my home place, Doneraile.

Another memory stirs, Granny waving us off, as her son Dinny drove a cartful of children to the point-to-point races in Annakisha, our journey a rattling, rumbling grandeur of sound punctuated by Neddy the donkey's breaking of wind. My father was a garda and I remember feeling as proud as a Doneraile peacock to see him directing traffic outside Mrs Griffin's Pub and calling Dinny and Neddy forward, like royalty at Ascot, to the head of the throng. You can't beat influence! Much lemonade was quaffed, a man was seen eating a rat, there was an escapologist and I was sick all the way home. Dinny was a most kindly man and often advised us not to believe all the stories adding, 'if the oul' lord hadn't died of the fox bite he might even be alive today'. Untackling and brushing down Neddy are among my happiest and earliest memories.

It seems curious that death was never far from my childhood, I remember when a man called Tom Carroll was killed out hunting with the Duhallows. He was laid out behind Tommo's Pub and the Gardai had to mind him. I remember bringing down tea to my father at night and he was very sombre. The Duhallows were and are a singular part of the life of north Cork and it was a great scene on an autumn morning to see the Reds, the Browns, the Greys and the Blues on their fine horses assembled for a stirrup cup outside Tommo's before they set off helter skelter across the countryside – the unspeakable in pursuit of the uneatable as Oscar Wilde might have said, but I doubt if they ever thought of that.

My father bought a sturdy black pony, which he called a cob, for my mother's family in East Cork. The Concise Oxford Dictionary defines 'cob' as being a 'sturdy short-legged horse'. She would from then until the end of her days be the bearer of the family to Sunday Mass and other chores such as carting dung or mangolds, or seaweed from the strand, or bringing water from the pump. Mollie, as she came to be known was a sweet-tempered and quiet animal, what Ted Walshe would call 'a decent horse'.

Now that she was bought, my father decided to ride her from Doneraile to Ballyshane in the parish of Cloyne, a journey of some 65 miles. I remember the smell of polished leather in the kitchen as saddle, reins and bridle were prepared and then he set off on his great adventure. Mollie and he completed the ride in great order and when he came home my father was full of tales of people he met, surprise in Garda stations he visited and the joy and welcome of my aunts and uncles when he reached journeys-end. I was very excited and proud of him because not everyone's father did that in those days and he gave me a ride on Mollie before he left.

My mother shook holy water on horse and rider, making the pony shudder. My father gave Mollie a few sugar lumps before he set off. She snickered with delight. He returned home in a much more mundane way, on the Newcastle West Bus. He carried the saddle over his shoulder as he arrived, looking, I thought, like the Durango Kid or Bill Boyd! Mollie was left to live out her life in her new home in east Cork.

I had by now another little sister, Mary, and I began to take a greater interest in the world around me. I suppose it was the picture house and the travelling shows that gave us the idea of performing plays ourselves. We generally 'performed' in an empty cell at the back of the Garda Station. Mrs O'Sullivan, the sergeant's wife, often rehearsed our songs at her piano and our mothers, fathers and friends whether or not they liked it, were our audience. We shared the pennies they gave us and the wartime childhood days of the early 1940s passed by in tranquillity. The sergeant, Tim O'Sullivan, a kindly and decent Kerryman was my godfather. I supposed it could be said that the local Garda families formed a little circle in themselves – the covered wagons of authority! Hanrahans, O'Sullivans, Nolans, O'Donnells and Dowlings were transients in the settled world of Doneraile.

Then my father was informed that he was to be transferred to Charleville just before Christmas. Consternation reigned. Sadness filled our little house. My mother was disconsolate. Goodbyes were tearful and anguished.

It was a most cruel time and seemed very unreasonable. My father was silent but I remember him walking down the garden in the winter-dusk as the crows flew home to roost. The priest said farewell to us from the pulpit. A lorry was loaded up with our possessions, shopkeepers and neighbours waved, the nuns gave my mother holy medals and promised prayers. It was a dreadful and brutal preparation for Christmas and a new life but as I looked out the back window in our hired car I knew in my child's mind that life, whether for better or for worse would never be the same again.

Doneraile left an indelible mark on me. The 'Gentle Mulla, the 'scaly trouts', the 'greedy pikes' of Edmund Spenser and the sound of convent bells evoke images of pastoral calm. The Doneraile of An tAthair Eoghan O Caoimh and An tAthair Peadar O Laoghaire, of Pat Pigott, the tailor remains with me through all the years.

Above all there is 'the Canon' and his rich and varied world of Munster during his days in my native village. Not too many know that Canon Sheehan loved Ireland with a deep and abiding passion; how acutely he observed what bloomed around him and made him write his own words to 'Seán O Duibhir a Ghleanna' in his novel *Glenanaar*.

> Long long we kept the hillside,
>
> Our couch hard by the rillside:
>
> The sturdy knotted oaken boughs
>
> Our canopy o'er head.
>
> The summer's heat we scoffed at,
>
> The winter's snow we laughed at:
>
> And trusted to our long, still swords
>
> To win us daily bread.

Indeed, this is what I learned from the late John Walshe of Laharn, who remembered especially 'the passion sermon.'

The Canon himself, was not unaware of his own powers, writing in 'Under the Cedars and the Stars,' he put it simply:

> Men go to hear the passion sermon who won't go to Mass. Protestants attend .... It must extend to an hour at least. Anything short of that is a disappointment ... Any departure from that is viewed with great displeasure by the people, "Twas a good sermon enough; but it was not a passion sermon" is the verdict.'

Whenever I think of Canon Sheehan and his grave in the Doneraile Churchyard, I look back in my mind's eye to the familiar headstone and its inscription:

> Gaze not, o stranger, with too curious eye
>
> Thou who art hostile, pass in silence by
>
> Friend, grant the tribute of a pleading tear
>
> Or benison on him who sleepeth here.

This was how my programme 'Canon Sheehan of Doneraile' ended on 22 November, 1964.

It was just 12 miles from Doneraile to Charleville but it might as well have been across the Atlantic. Doneraile was the place of my birth and now as I left it I felt all the sadness of the emigrant.

Although I didn't know it then, the best of times lay just ahead. But as we crossed over the Awbeg River, Canon Sheehan's old house was the last we saw of Doneraile in 1943, the end of childhood in one life. As I write this now in 1998 I am hard-put to express my feelings. The poet Padraig J. Daly says it well as he invites us into his childhood, not unlike my own ...

> But it was the Canon who reared our imaginations most of all,
>
> and taught us love for the quiet about us,
>
> The green calm (unbroken by any sea)
>
> Of Muskerry fields and the dogs barking at foxes at evening.

The Best Of Times

'Charleville', said the hackney man as the two spires came into view and on 14 December 1943 I first saw my new home. Having left behind us our neighbours' tears, we arrived in our new home town. My mother was distraught, my father seemed very sad and we, my two sisters and myself, were too young to really understand the trauma of our parents. Here was a new place, new friends and a new life where I would spend what proved to be the happiest days of my boyhood and young manhood. But that was all to come.

For now, we were moving into a 'flat', a foreign aspect of living when there was no garden, no high walls, no demesne, no pigeons, just streets at front and back. We lived over Binchy's Bread Shop which provided not just gloriously fresh bread but smells that rose up into our apartment filling the air with aromas that fostered appetites and have ever since given the taste and smell of fresh bread a special place in my life.

We had one very large living room, the corners of which seemed always in shadow. The windows were large and provided a panoramic view of the main street and all that happened there. The first shock in our new life was the amalgam of sound and vision when the quiet of early morning was broken by the mournful lowing and bellowing of cattle announcing the noisy beginnings of the Charleville monthly cattle fair. This event was held in the main street. Beast and man mingled from early morning until early afternoon as farmer, drover, dealer, townsperson and animal shared the main street and strove to keep their bovine charges from entering business premises and private homes.

Christmas 1943 was a lonely time. It was wartime and Christmas presents, Christmas cards, and all such fripperies were almost unheard of. I was given a present of a book, *Glenanaar* by Canon Sheehan who I mentioned in the last chapter as having lived in Doneraile. This is a novel which has remained with me ever since and which seems to capture the life of north Cork before and during the Canon's time.

Christmas morning meant early Mass in the parish church and quiet wishes for 'Happy Christmas', although, these were few and far between as we were, after all, strangers in a strange place. The Christmas lunch consisted of a goose which came in by post a few days earlier, carefully but ineffectively wrapped by my country cousins, causing the postman to say to my mother, 'I'd cook that soon missus,' which she did and it tasted absolutely splendid. As far as I can remember, we had no Christmas tree. They didn't seem to be in fashion at that time but late on Christmas Eve my father lit two Christmas candles in each of the big windows facing onto the main street and their flame curled up straight and mysterious into the dark reaches of the ceiling of our new home. He brought us out to the street to look up at the windows and to admire his handiwork saying that it reminded him of Christmas and home. Like I said, it was nostalgic and lonely. The local choir sang the 'Adeste Fideles' during Mass and we were brought to the crib, which was quite different to the one in Doneraile. The figures here were full size and looked very real in the dim light and in the straw. Later, a camel, which stood outside the crib, and three wise men were brought to lend a majesty to a simple and telling scene. I had never seen a camel, not even an artificial one before and harboured a great desire to climb up on the camel's back which I did some years later only to be discovered by Canon Burke who administered a not-too-hefty kick on the backside as he told me, 'don't be desecrating holy places'.

January 1944 brought another new experience: going to school for the first time in Charleville. This was a Christian Brothers school where Eamon de Valera and Archbishop Mannix of Melbourne both attended. I knew because both of their pictures were in the hallway. The Brother who met me decided that I should go into third class which was then taught by Mr Davey O'Riordan, whose wife Statia had a pub across the road from our flat, and where I often had a surreptitious bottle of lemonade – my mother did not hold with her first-born entering pubs! Davey was a good teacher because I remember much of what he taught me. I remember, in particular, the poems we learned, 'Brian Boru's Address To His Army Before The Battle Of Clontarf' and which begins with the ringing order

Stand ye now for Eireann's glory, Stand ye now for Eireann's cause,

Long ye've groaned beneath the rigours of northman's savage laws.

I learned this with great gusto and often said it to myself out loud in bed at night. The other poem which I remember seemed to be called 'Shane The Proud's Reply To Queen Elizabeth' which told the story of Shane O'Neill's formal statement to the Queen of England when declining whatever it was she offered him.

I scorn your lady's honour, I scorn her titles vain,

A prince am I of high degree and of a fair domain.

I really love the lines when he said, 'I am a King in Kingly right and hold my Kingdom free'.

Davey was never at his best in the mornings after dances. We always knew this was so when he took off his coat, barely looked at us and said 'take out your books and learn a page of spellings' and then proceeded to close his eyes and doze for a few minutes. We loved the mornings after dances.

Brother Ryan was another who captured my attention and remains firmly in my memory. He taught us Irish and not just the language but a love of it. I liked in particular, and this seems unusual, learning the declensions, when declensions were really declensions when masculine was masculine and feminine was really feminine as in the case of the first and second declensions.

How can one forget the joys of 'an fear – hata an fhir – na fir – hataí na bhfear – leis na fearaibh' or the feminine delights of 'an bhean – hata na mná (genitive singular) – hataí na mban (genitive plural) – leis na mnaibh'. Now it seems to be all the same, singular, plural, nominative and genitive all one untidy over-simplistic, patronising mess. God be with the good old days.

Brother Ryan also trained the school hurling team. Now, I was never a star turn on that side and all the time I spent dreaming of scoring goals and making winning speeches was to no avail because, with my spectacles, I couldn't see beyond the next player and the ball was only a small blur that sometimes hit me in the face. I once played at right half back in a hurling match in Kilmallock and in a frenzy of excitement and no little skill struck my own full back in the forehead and was asked to leave the field, which I refused to do, and which proved the end of a none too promising career. In a fit of pique, I didn't travel back to Charleville with the rest of the team in the back of a truck but drove back in style, eating an ice-cream, in Davey Ryan's hearse. I rarely think of my next such trip.

Hobbies were simple – catching 'collies' (sticklebacks) in the river, bird nesting along 'the double ditch' beyond Love Lane and tormenting decent, courting couples who were endeavouring to go about their romantic business. It's amazing how quickly a deftly thrown sod of grass can terminate the warmest and most passionate embrace, never mind cooling the ardour of seemingly respectable French kissers whom we often discovered at dusk and at whom we would shout, 'we'll tell your mother, you dirty thing', only to be pursued by a distraught lover shouting 'go home you little bastards, I'll break your necks if I catch ye', hastily hitching up his galluses as he ran. It was difficult to meet these gentlemen and ladies on the way to Mass on Sundays and to look them in the eye without shouting the Charleville word for lovers – 'nobber'. It must have been 30 years later that I was compering a concert in Hunter College, New York when a voice from the back end of the balcony shouted 'nobber' as I came on the stage. I knew what he meant and he knew too. We had a great pint later.

Serving Mass in Charleville was a formal affair. We wore red soutanes, because, true or false, one of the curates was a doctor of divinity named Dr Browne, DD, a relative of the now-famous Fr Browne, the *Titanic* photographer, who was a very noisy man in the confession. Once as I sat outside the box preparing for my weekly outpouring of sins, I heard him shout at a friend of mine, 'get out, get out, you're the makings of a great blackguard'. My friend emerged from the box looking very red-faced and looking around to see if his mother was at the back of the church. She wasn't. The same Dr Browne had a stentorian voice which he used to great effect from the pulpit as he looked down to see who was standing at the back of the church during Mass. In urging them to approach the table of the Lord he would address them in such tones, 'come up from behind the pillar and let me see your face. Seats are for sitting in and there's no extra charge'.

Dr Browne, who had been a chaplain in the First World War, had a particular dislike for chaps who knelt on one knee behind the pillars and would say, 'come out, come out, you one-eyed gunners'. They invariably retreated.

Canon Burke was the parish priest, a nice holy man of his time and therefore a bit severe. I remember one Sunday distributing Holy Communion with him, I carried the paten, when a lady approached the altar rails wearing lipstick and slacks. The Canon paused in full flight, and said very loudly 'Madam, take off that thing off your lips and take off your trousers – we'll have no women wearing those in the house of the Lord'. She also retreated. The next person along the way was one of my friends from the 'double ditch'.

Charleville also offered me new excitements. I had never seen nuns walking the streets in Doneraile. The Presentation Sisters were an enclosed congregation while the Mercy Sisters in Charleville were not and walked out 'on visitation' but always in pairs. Mother Francis was in charge of the choir which I joined because, like everyone else about me, I thought I was a little special, having a good voice. Anyway there were some nice girls in the choir and I liked looking at them at practice on

Tuesday nights. The fact that my voice had hardly broken did not concern me because when the nun asked me what kind of voice I had, I said 'bass'. Whether or not she was surprised when I sang in a somewhat high-pitched semi-tenor, she never said. By the way, Sister Imelda who played the organ always rendered 'Moonlight and Roses' before Benediction. She once asked a well-known local character to leave when he sang 'The Wild Colonial Boy' during the 'Tantum Ergo'. He sold music broadsheets and thought, I suppose, to promote his wares.

The first night that I ever saw Eamon de Valera he came to Charleville to address a public meeting. It was an event in the grand old style, tar barrels blazing, cheering, waving, great excitement and Dev in his long black coat addressing the crowd without a microphone. I climbed up the side of the truck and managed to catch his hand and was about to address him when a large garda who happened to be my father, and was acutely embarrassed, bore down on me and told me, somewhat impolitely that he would 'see me at home'. I knew what he meant. Being a guard's son gave one certain responsibilities, reasons for being especially good, like not hurling on the street and certainly not climbing into the pony traps outside the Church on Sunday. But before I left I managed to shake the hand of Sean Moylan and asked him for his autograph. He was surprised and said, not unkindly, 'have a bit of sense for yourself, little boy', which I hadn't and some would say never had. Another day, I saw James Dillon address a meeting from the steps of the Imperial Hotel. He had no microphone either and it was on a fair day. Between the lowing of the cows, the shouting of the drovers, and the general mayhem I don't know how he made himself heard, but he did because a few Fianna Fáilers near me said 'that fella'd deafen you'.

After a year or so in Charleville we moved to a real house in 'The Turrets' next to the Parish Church. Our neighbours, generally kind, made us welcome. Miss Spillane, a national teacher, lived next door and would play a fairly central role in my life later on, when I joined the Legion of Mary.

Others whom I remember were John and Mrs Horan. She had, as far as I can remember, been housekeeper to Bishop O'Dwyer, the famous nationalist Bishop of Limerick. Tom Burke and his family lived further down and it was in their house that I listened on the wireless to Dev's reply to Winston Churchill after the war.

These were the days of the LSF (Local Security Forces) and the LDF (Local Defence Forces) when the young men of Ireland answered de Valera's call and prepared to defend the country against the enemy, be it

German or British. The LSF were unarmed and generally older than the LDF who carried weapons and seemed to be always marching. One of our neighbours was a member of the LSF and would often march down the road after drill out of tune and out of step, 'bawling' The Soldier's Song.

Tom Carey, the sacristan, was a great friend of mine and often allowed us to climb the narrow stairs up to the belfry to ring the Angelus bell. My mother felt that Tom was a saint and maybe he was. When he died there was a great local outcry to have him buried in the Chapel yard alongside the priests. The Canon, whether or not he was sympathetic to the wishes of the public, resisted and Tom was laid to rest among all the neighbours in the cemetery.

* * *

By late 1946, my life was about to change forever. My father became seriously unwell and was confined to bed. He seemed to recover early in 1947 and during the dreadful snows of that winter, I remember him reading an account to us of the shipwreck of the *SS Irish Plane* on the Ballyshane coast of East Cork. I told boys in school that I knew the place which I did, adding that I knew the captain, too, which I did not! I do know, however, that the pigs on my uncle's farm feasted during these days as the scrapping team on the ship bought potatoes, cabbage and more from the locals. The pigs fed on the leftovers which were paid in kind.

My father's life was almost over and on a sunny May evening he died. It was, in fact, 22 May 1947 and I was with him at the end. I can never forget the stillness of the room, the laboured breathing and the kindly nun who prayed for him. An uncle of mine from Kerry fussed ineffectually and crudely in the breathless room. I touched his hand but there was no response. He was in his fifty-first year and I have never ceased to miss him. His passing turned a little boy into 'the eldest of the family, and a hope for the future for your mother'. I could say much more of this but even after all the years I find it inexpressibly sad and too personal to put on paper. Indeed writing about it has conjured up strange dreams and dark memories when I came closer than I have ever come since to the 'other side' and the hoped-for brightness of eternity.

My mother was never the same again and mourned my father until her own death in the 1970s. The cold spirit of death had confronted me as never before and, I am glad to say, as never since. Certain outward effects should be mentioned. I met my Kerry relations and heard the chilling Kerry *Caoine* for the first and only time.

Saying 'goodbye' was formal, a nervous kiss planted on cold and icy lips, a touch of hands, neither warm nor familiar, and the unspeakable fear of the dark cowl on the shroud pulled down across my father's deathly, unmoving face. All this time, my mother clung to his hand until she was turned away and we left the dead room where there was nothing left of the father I loved and cannot forget.

Changes were fast and stark. A garda came to the door to demand my father's notebook, a treasured heirloom, much cherished by the young widow. The state also removed the uniform that hung in the wardrobe and even some buttons left on my mother's dressing table. It was all dreadfully cruel. I do not know if they treat Garda widows in that way nowadays. I hope not.

During the summer of 1947, our radio was silent, silent and covered with a black cloth. I went in next door to Miss Spillane to listen to the matches. A tall Presentation Brother from Cork called to our door. A local man had suggested to my mother that I might like to go away to school for a few years. Indeed, it would be one less mouth to feed and would lead me on to secondary education. She agreed. My vocation was guaranteed. The tall Brother told tall tales of swimming pools, trips to the seaside with hints of 'taking the habit and great times ahead'.

I was swept along on a tide of optimism and soon two black suits were purchased, shirts, socks and a red football jersey, a hurley and a daily missal. Excitement knew no bounds. My east Cork relations did not seem to be consulted. I was told 'your father is looking down on you, he must be a happy man today'.

Finally, the day came and I left Charleville on the bus. My mother cried again, another parting. I only drew breath when we came to Passage West to the juniorate for the Presentation Brothers, where there was no swimming pool.

The early nights were spent in sobbing loneliness when the only noise was provided by my companion weeping. Sadness was plentiful. But I settled. The Brothers, especially Br De Sales were kind and the boys were only too anxious to be friendly. Br Aenghus, the Superior, seemed to have one ambition in life – to uproot every ailing tree stump in the college grounds. With our unwilling help he achieved most of his hopes.

Sunday Mass was an event. We walked in ordered pairs to the parish church in Passage and it was here on the fourteenth Sunday after Pentecost that we first heard the magnificent voice of Fr Seamus O'Flynn. Although I did not know it then, he was the man who had taught drama, particularly Shakespeare, to many of the greatest Cork actors and actresses of our generation in a little theatre, 'The Loft' in the northside of Cork City. He was now parish priest of Passage West and it would be my honour and exciting privilege to listen to him for a year or so.

Anyway, on this particular Sunday he roared into top gear. His text was from the gospel according to St Matthew and the words, magnificent and mellifluous, soared into every corner of the church. There was no microphone.

'Consider the lilies of the field, how they grow, they labour not, neither do they spin; but I say to you, that now even Solomon in all his glory was never arrayed as one of these'.

He then drew apposite analogies between the simple requirements of the 'birds of the air' and the lilies and various members of his congregation, most notably, 'the brilliantine boys whose locks run wet around their ears as they stand inattentive and preening unheeding at this Divine sacrifice in this lovely Church'. His sermon concluded with the colourful advice to 'seek ye first the kingdom of God, and his justice; and all these things shall be added unto you'.

We then stood for the creed, which he, and those of us who knew it, sang. I was transfixed with excitement. It gave new meanings to Sunday Mass and there was more to follow. Later in that week we had our confessions heard by Fr O'Flynn and here he was as colourful as everywhere else. When we had concluded the business side of the operation, he turned towards me and asked where I was from. I told him and he said 'Aha bhuachaill, Sean Clárach MacDomhnaill, Ard Shiriam na Mumhan' and proceeded to sing or intone 'Bím-se Buan'. The 'high sheriff' Mac Domhnaill was chief of the poets of the River Maigue. 'Bím-se buan' begins a poem lamenting the departure of the 'young pretender' and regretting the passing of the Stuart dynasty. He then asked me if I liked Shakespeare.

I said, 'yes I do Father, Henry the Fourth, Part One', which was on the Intermediate Certificate Course for that year.

'I must call up to St Teresa's during the week', he said and told me to say one Hail Mary for his and my own intentions.

Monday mornings were never my favourite times. Br Aenghus presided over mathematics and, in particular, over geometry when the world of theorems interrupted the fairly even tenor of my schooldays. Not alone did I fail to understand them but I hated them with every fibre of my being. This particular Monday, however, changed all of that. Fr O'Flynn arrived or rather, he seemed to materialise through the great French window exclaiming without preamble 'so shaken as we art, so wan with care', the opening lines of Henry IV Part 1.

Br Aenghus was not best amused. We were enthralled not to say relieved. So it was on many a morning that the great Shakespearean scholar led us on a magical journey through the words and works of the Bard of Avon. We – those of us who wished to – grew to know and love the character of Falstaff, young Harry Hotspur, Prince Hal and all the others. Fr O'Flynn breathed life into the word as he brought his own brand of realistic interpretation to Shakespeare. Every character grew, every nuance was cherished, every theme, every word came to life. The final soliloquy of Henry IV, Scene I Act 1 is still with me, 'I know you all and will awhile uphold the unyoked humour of your idleness'.

The Irish language as the lingua franca of our schooldays was prised open and thrust living and loved before us. Characters from Pearse's loving stories, like Brighid na nAmhrán and Eoghainín na nÉan spoke to us and we understood them. Fr O'Flynn and the Presentation Brothers opened up to us new compositions of thinking and of feeling.

I wheeled and dealed my way, often unwisely, through the educational system; I often wrote four essays on the same topic for companions while they 'did' algebra and geometric problems for me. All too soon the Inter Cert year passed and I spent the next nine months in Mount St Joseph's Novitiate above Blarney Street in Cork City.

Life was more ascetic here. It was early to bed and early to rise in a severe but never unkind regime. I remember the long summer evenings when, after we retired to our beds at 9 p.m., we heard the voices of children playing in the streets and longed for our friends at home. We rose at 5.30 a.m. and trooped in single file 'without running' to the chapel for meditation and Mass. It was all beyond me, especially the constant warnings against 'particular friendships' and the absolute need for 'custody of the eyes' and being advised how to shake hands modestly with a young woman. I never seemed to meet anyone with whom to shake hands!

The shock of cold mornings as I splashed my face with icy water gave a new meaning to Leigh Hunt's 'Getting up in Cold Mornings', an essay that much appealed to my own experience. Reading was fairly confined. Apart from a surreptitious glance at the sports pages of the *Cork Examiner* on Mondays, our only reading came from the lives of the saints and even these were somewhat proscribed. St Gabriel the Passionist's life was removed from the library. He was a young man with a penchant for self-flagellation who was copied by one of my confreres, much to the fear of those who listened to his attempts at self-mortification and to the annoyance of our master of novices. The book was subsequently removed from the library. I loved the reading at meal times and, surprise, surprise, particularly enjoyed my own reading! A biography of the heroic Fr Willie Doyle SJ, a chaplain who was killed during World War One, the life of Dominic Savio, stories of St Patrick and the bible were much favoured.

I was always impressed by the older Brothers, people like old Br Martin who spent hours in the church. They were gentle, unworldly people and when the time came for me to leave them I was sad. I knew, however, that this was not the life for me and so, one day, after much heart-searching, I asked to see Br Benignus, the Master of Novices, and informed him of my intentions. He listened to me in silence, asked if I was certain and when I said I was, he shook my hand and said a swift goodbye.

My clothes and few books were quickly packed, a taxi was ordered and quite quickly, without any goodbyes, I was whisked away to the bus station and, with £5 in my pocket was returned to where I came from. It was sad not to say goodbye but I must say that I look back with thanks and nostalgia to the Presentation Brothers who helped to mould that part of my life.

* * *

Charleville was as if I had never left it and my mother, if she was disappointed in me certainly did not show it. I was warmly welcomed back into the family and the family home at 45 Holy Cross Place where we now lived. There was one problem. It was insisted that I 'wear out' my black suit, which I did but it's difficult when you're fifteen and a half years old to be 'different', but soon I merged back with my peers.

Money was always scarce at home. Mouths had to be fed and the time had come for me to go to work. I was 16 years old when I began my apprenticeship as a dental technician with Paddy O'Riordan, the dentist in Charleville. A new phase had begun when I thought that I had said goodbye forever to books and studies. My conditions of employment were not unduly onerous. My salary, five shillings a week for the first six months was hardly excessive although it increased to ten shillings after that. John Morrison was already employed there as dental technician and I found him kind, if a little remote. Paddy, the dentist, was a man of great kindness and before long he gave me access to his extensive library and I began reading the detective stories of Agatha Christie and Edgar Wallace, in particular the story of 'Educated Evans', and the works of John. D. Sheridan. I was also given a read of the *Irish Press* every day which suited me well. The wireless was also brought downstairs to the little workshop to enable us to hear any rugby internationals on Saturdays. Paddy purchased the *Reader's Digest* every month and often 'examined' me in the 'Increase Your Wordpower' page.

One of my regular trips was to Doneraile on Thursdays, my half-day. I would stop at the bridge of the Awbeg River and think of *Glenanaar* and Canon Sheehan. On summer evenings, I often cycled to and from hurling matches in Mallow. My companion was Bill Galligan, a neighbour in Holy Cross Place. Bill was no mean hurler himself and hurled until his forties, a man of warmth and friendliness, he seemed to change on the hurling field. He once told me that, 'I see red when I see that ball'. His son Billy, who now lives in Limerick, played hurling with Blackrock and Cork while his grandson Mike is a classic hurling forward with the Limerick senior team. The long summer evenings were well filled. Talk was always of hurling for which the north Cork countryside provided a living backdrop.

Walking to and from the railway station was one of the great evening avocations of my boyhood. Noel Tarrant, who lived in a large old house on Broad Street, was a particular friend. He had a collection of 78 rpm records. We loved to listen to Richard Tauber, Josef Locke, Al Jolson, The Andrews Sisters and songs like 'The Tennessee Waltz'.

Soccer began to appeal and Noel got a programme from Manchester every second week when Manchester United played at home. Now and again, when we could afford it, we went to matches in the Mardyke in Cork to see Cork Athletic play. This was another new world and brought us new heroes – Florrie Burke, a great centre half and Paddy O'Leary, a peerless centre forward with a great head! I also saw Raich Carter play his first game for Cork Athletic against Waterford. He scored from a penalty kick. Wingate was the Waterford goalkeeper. We often put a few shillings on the horses, hoping to win money to pay our fare to Cork. I don't think we ever did.

At this time, I was a constant letter writer to the stars, indeed, I have never ceased to be a fan. I quickly acquired a collection of autographed photographs, Jo Stafford of the silken voice, Ronnie Ronald, the whistler, Donald Peers, Robert Wilson the Scottish tenor, Tommy Moroney, who played soccer for West Ham, Derek Roy, the radio comedian and the most surprising of all, Peter Desmond, a young Corkman who played at inside forward for Middlesbrough.

Peter, who came from Evergreen Street in Cork, was an ex-army man who played for Shelbourne and was quickly transferred across the water with Arthur Fitzsimons. He was chosen on the famous Irish soccer team, victors over England 2–0 in Goodison Park, Liverpool in 1949. He and I exchanged letters on a weekly basis for a whole season. Through him I procured autographs of many of the famous 'Boro players of the time;- Wilf Mannion, one of the greatest forwards of his generation, George Hardwick, England full-back and captain. These were glorious times for a young fan and his letters and programmes were shown to many of my friends in Charleville. I met Peter just once. When the train stopped at the station on a summer evening, he and I shook hands, said hello and then goodbye and never met again. He slipped out of football with teams like Southport and York while I returned to the mundane but real world of Charleville.

I drifted into the Legion of Mary, more from boredom than anything else and attended weekly meetings, at first in the Christian Brothers school and later in the sacristy of the parish church. Maybe future events were casting long shadows but I attempted to have our meetings conducted in Irish. This was very well until adult members came to visit and failed to comprehend the business in hand. I soon became a member of the Senior Presidium. Among those attending was Canon Burke who was Spiritual Director.

We were shocked and some were galvanised by the visit of a Dublin legionary. This enthusiastic young man seemed intent on 'spreading the word of the Lord' and I was consigned to be his companion and guide. I was not much amused. Anyway, one Thursday, my half-day when I would normally have spent my time cleaning the headstone of the poet Seán Clárach MacDomhnaill in the local cemetery, I set off with my guest to the village of Newtownshandrum. I chose this village as I thought that it would be deserted by mid-afternoon and so my friend was quite unlikely to meet anyone. I borrowed two ladies bicycles and we set off. All went well until we arrived in the village and my friend jumped off the bicycle and sprinted towards the denizens of the street corner. He sprang to introductions, 'this is my friend Denis Dowling and I'm ...'.

One lively local looked me up and down and said, 'how's it goin', Cove, what's the crack?'

Before I could reply, they were asked a straight question. 'Do you know Jesus?'

The reply was equally straight, 'Christ, what kind of lunatics have we here?' looking me hard in the eye. My companion was undeterred. Prayer was the answer.

'Let's say some prayers', as he headed towards the church.

I followed. Now I had never prayed out loud in church without a priest present, but I was unhinged and we were half-way through the first decade of the sorrowful mysteries when Fr Mortell, the parish priest exploded into the church. 'What do you think you're doing here on a quiet Thursday afternoon? You'd be better off taking God's fresh air and not disturbing decent people'. He looked at me. 'I know you, young Dowling. Go home to Charleville for yourself'.

We did. Less than an hour later, I was summoned to the Parochial House. The Canon was red-faced. 'You don't need to explain,' he said. 'Our young gentleman guest will be on the Dublin train later this evening. There is no more to say'.

The weekly meetings were presided over by Jim Burke, the station master: Tom Daly from Ballyhea, Pat Gray, TJ MacCurtain and my great friend and advisor Michael McGrath were among others who attended. Michael and I spent some hours each week on 'Legion Work' when we distributed 'spiritual booklets', chosen by the Canon, to a none-too-interested public. The modus operandi was simple. The books were handed in and sometime, a week or two later, we returned to discuss the contents with them. Michael, being a postman and a gentle man was known and loved so we were invited in for tea and Michael stated sensibly, 'you enjoyed the book then, Missus?'

The reply was usually the same, 'Oh yes, Mr McGrath very much. We're always delighted when yourself and young Denis call around'. Young Denis had by now spotted our book behind the wireless in company with several other Legion offerings of the recent past.

So, Saturday afternoons passed, gently and kindly among our neighbours and Michael McGrath introduced me to the joys of visiting and friendly conversation. We held our meetings on Monday night and reported on our visits to the Praesidium (the name of each branch). Everyone was referred to as 'brother'.

Michael McGrath always began his report in his own unobtrusive and optimistic way. 'Great success again this week, Canon. Brother Dowling and I delivered books in the Broghill area and the general reaction was good. Our books are much cherished.'

He would then nod in my direction and my contribution was invariably the same, 'Oh, yes indeed, very successful'. The Canon expressed great delight and offered the opinion that 'a good book is always worth reading more than once'. With such aphoristic comment we passed onto the next report, but not before TJ MacCurtain offered a cryptic comment, 'oh yes, Canon, it's always nice to get the tea. You can't beat a nice drink in the middle of the day.' He then sat back and looked forward to calling in again to Miss Reidy's or John R's premises on his way home. His face looked suffused with virtue!

Mainchín Seoighe from Bruree often gave talks on the Irish language in the old national school. I attended and before long was an enthusiastic member of the Gaelic League. I organised a drama group, 'The Gaelic League Players', and shortly afterwards we were performing in the Parochial Hall and in other villages around the countryside. I really fancied myself! I persuaded my employer, Paddy O'Riordan to compere the concerts. He did this in style, always wearing a dress suit. One of the plays was *Fledged and Flown*, an early work in which Bryan MacMahon collaborated. We performed at the first North Cork Drama Festival at which Bryan was adjudicator. We did not win but we certainly shocked Bryan. As he said, 'it was like going to Ballybunion with your wife and family and meeting there a girl that you once kissed thirty years ago', meaning that he was startled, surprised, but not a little delighted to see one of his earlier works on stage. The Gaelic League now took up more and more of my time and with the generous help of Diarmuid O'Donncha, a young man who worked in the post office and gave me books to read in Irish, I discovered a new world.

At this time I was invited to sell a magazine called *Rosc* in the streets of Charleville and soon discovered that not everyone in the town shared my enthusiasm for the language and the Republican ideals that went with it. I dealt with a group from Limerick and through them I met Seán South and with my usual penchant for writing letters I soon made contact with Sinn Féin and received my copy of *The United Irishman* through the post. This paper seemed confidential to myself until one day the postman raised the flap of the letter box and shouted: 'Listen, Cove when you finish with that, give us a read!' Around this time I decided to take my beliefs and aspirations a little farther, I travelled to Cork to join the IRA.

The young lady in charge of the rooms I visited was not impressed. 'I'd like to join the IRA', I said.

'They're gone home to their tea', she replied. 'Call back tomorrow'.

I had reached a stone wall. 'I won't be in the city, I'm from the country', was my reply.

She was unmoved, 'I'm sorry, that's too bad'. That was the end of the story. I returned to Charleville and never again attempted to join the movement. Of such accidents of time are revolutions frustrated!

* * *

By now my activities had spread to organising céilithe with such as 'The Vincent Lowe Trio', whose accordionist was a young Dermot O'Brien and 'The Malachy Sweeney Ceili Band', with singer Anna Boyle in the Pavilion Cinema, not to mention eight o'clock 'til midnight hops in the Parochial Hall with 'The Tostal Ceili Band' from Mallow or the 'Shandrum Ceili Band' from Newtownshandrum.

The Parochial Hall Committee, which fostered the playing of billiards, innocent card games, (gambling not countenanced!) listening to the wireless in our Radio Room, and organising 'Celebrity Concerts', was now in its prime and I was appointed secretary. My employer, Paddy O'Riordain, was Chairman and Fr Linehan was President. We embarked on two major events, a Celebrity Concert held in the Parochial Hall on 14 February 1954 and a 'Monster Céilí' in the Pavilion Cinema with Jimmy Shand and his band. The latter event never occurred. This was a long story and through no fault of ours, it never happened!

I was wildly excited about the concert and decided to have my voice trained! Michael Murphy and Terry Cashman, two splendid singers from Cobh, were more than helpful and recommended their teacher, Kate O'Connor, as most suitable, that is, if she found my voice worth training. She did and that's another story but before we come to it I would like to take you back to the Parochial Hall in Charleville and its influence on my life.

Membership of the Parochial Hall Billiard Club cost £1 per year, which amount was acceptable in any number of ways. We had two very splendid billiard tables, well patronised and the pride and joy of our members who like myself were mostly working class. I kept records of all our members. Paddy Troy was sometime caretaker while Paddy Sheridan, known as 'the King' because of his prowess at billiards, was among our stars. There was another club, the Commercial Club, which catered for solicitors, bank clerks, doctors, vets and some shopkeepers. They were our deadly rivals and I well remember when we defeated them in a tournament. It gave off strange echoes of the Russian revolution!

* * *

Hurling was and is the great enduring sport in north Cork and there was no way that a young lad in the 1950s could not but be impressed. After my earlier experiences as tyro hurler I quickly realised that I was meant to be a spectator and so, my first Munster Hurling Final was certain to be remembered.

My Munster final memories are locked into conflict between two counties; they span the 1950s and concern the counties of Cork and

Tipperary. I suppose their importance to me springs from the fact that they were my first finals and remain forever etched between the sharp parameters of late boyhood and early manhood.

Days seem always tinged with gold, ripe indeed with new-mown hay and warmed with the memories of times when hurling, and hurling only, filled our hearts. These were days when I joined my cousins in the sweet smelling hayfields of east Cork where conversations, those of my elders of course, spanned the hurling decades and when the sun burned young and unready shoulders with its searing summer rays. These were nights, too, when my aunt coated fevered skin with cream from the dairy or even with buttermilk which was often quite effective against the depredations of the sun.

All day long, from the early morning milking until that of the late evening our lives were framed by the hayfields and our hearts by hurling, conversations which were often supplemented by our communal evening study of the hurling page in the *Cork Examiner*. Cork and Tipperary hurlers flitted here and there in blue and gold and red and white splendour, as they shared between them the epic successes of a special time.

These were days when the clatter and the rattle of the mowing machine followed the almost silent stepping of the horses from headland to headland, ending in the mid-field, frightened scamper of rabbits and birds hopefully evading death by knife-edged inches. It would soon be time for talking to begin. A silence fell, to be broken only by the grass-munching horses or the delicate chant of some high-flying skylarks contending with the numerous lazy songs of the long summer days of boyhood. The oldsters looked appreciatively at another fine crop of hay while the youngsters looked forward to the rattle of mug and teapot when the mid-morning sustenance would break the silence. Men and women sat back, pipes were lit and cigarettes puffed, while the horses lazily flicked away some rapacious horse flies.

My aunt would issue her regular warning not to be 'roasted alive' and the adults, smug veterans of many burnings, but now well clad for heat, set about turning the hay, preparing it for a later cocking. No matter how fine the day, inevitable questions were asked. 'Will it last?' with the odd squint towards the sun or the Atlantic ocean that shimmered and glittered some three fields away. Ger Ryan would lazily remark, 'no, there's no change'. Other more important questions intervened, 'who'll win on Sunday?' No reply. The question was rhetorical.

Anyway there were no doubts in the minds of boyhood, disappointment had not yet found a place among us. Heroes, and we had our share, were always victorious in that strange world of boyhood.

My hay-making days were always spent in the postal district of Ballyshane, Cloyne, Co. Cork, and inevitably, Christy Ring entered the learned conjectures of hayfield tea-breaks. Haycock or headland were forum for lively and often knowledgeable discussion. Those who remembered constantly discussed the merits of the great Cloyneman with those of a great hurling hero of earlier times, Jamesy Kelliher from Dungourney and almost always the horse-riding hurler from earlier times emerged the victor. In our world of hayfield seers, the present had no chance.

More recent times, like the war years of the 1940s were remembered with delight. Nostalgia for the 'bicycle Munster finals' knew no bounds. Stories of cycle tyres filled with hay were only surpassed by the length of time it took, measured in days, to cycle from east Cork to Thurles which was made to sound as crowded and as colourful as the old medieval pilgrim routes to Santiago de Compostela. Mick Mackey, his brother John and Paddy Scanlon, the goalkeeper, came hurling down the leafy lanes of time, while Mick surged on eternal and flamboyant as he soloed through great swathes of memory.

Lory Meagher from Tullaroan was another who entered our lists. Ned Hanley said that someone had compared his hurling style to the grace of a swallow. Another who once went as far as Croke Park in the 1930s never forgot it.

Magical names filled the hayfield. Dinny Barry Murphy, Sean Óg Murphy, Ronayne from Dungourney, you always needed one hard man, Ga and Balty Aherne from Blackrock, Fox Collins from the Glen, Batty Thornhill, the only barber in Buttevant, and many more in our long litany of Cork heroes.

There were other welcome distractions in the hayfield as when Jack Creamer, the postman from Cloyne cycled round the Croisairín and dropped in for tea and the 'latest news' from the Cork camp. Without being asked he would volunteer, 'he was down last night ... great form ... hurley in the car ... said that Willie John was all set ... a few of them Tipp lads might be injured ... ah yes ... there's no doubt about Sunday', and away he went whistling, heading towards Curtins to deliver some post and to carefully avoid the gander. He always brightened our day and was considered to talk 'straight from the horse's mouth!'

We often had a visit from the 'Fish Man' from Ballycotton who had news that 'a famous hurling priest of other years was holidaying in Ballymacoda with his mother'. He never said his name. My aunt, who hadn't much time for hurling chat, enquired if he had any ling. He had and we would be thirsty until next week. Before leaving, he informed us that 'Gerry White's van will be here soon with *The Cork Weekly Examiner*, although there's no good news in it.' With a flick of the reins, his parting shot was to say the least unhelpful, 'Tipp are quite hopeful you know. It might be their day at last'. There was a long silence and productivity soared in his trotting wake. 'What would he know about hurling anyhow?' What indeed?

My first journey to a Munster Hurling Final took two days. We travelled in a small Ford, compact, reliable, sturdy, bone-shaking and very slow. My cousin Maurice took the wheel, my Uncle Jim (really Maurice's father) sat in the back while I, being from Charleville and knowing the way, sat in great excitement in the front seat.

Preparations for the epic journey were carefully discussed after the tea when long summer dusks lingered and merged into purple Munster twilights, when the oil lamp was lit in the kitchen, when bellows urged on the furze and sticks to a gentle glow while outside, the hens, complaining sleepily, were tucked up for the night and sparrows and swallows nestled under the thatch to the raucous accompaniment of gander and geese on their protesting way to day's end.

The car was in the barn, quiet, washed, shined, ready and waiting. The rug on the back seat was the only sign that a journey was contemplated. Sandwiches of the ham and chicken variety were discussed. Lemonade, water and two bottles of stout were considered, not to mention home-made favours in red and white. I even suggested a newspaper picture of Christy Ring for my lapel. That was rejected as being too 'smart' and, anyway, my aunt said twas a bit of a cheek when I didn't even know the man.

The Friday night was almost unbearable. The rosary, all five sorrowful mysteries seemed interminable, not to mention 'the trimmings' including the 'Hail Holy Queen' and a veritable litany for 'special favours'. Prayers for journeys and holy purity (I do not know what they expected) were added for good measure. Uncle Jim said he had not prayed as much since he was up the Dardanelles during World War One. My aunt said, 'have sense for yourself and don't start about the war!' For better or for worse anyway, he had no choice for I asked him to tell me how the Turk cut off the head of the Englishman. My aunt clucked as yet again we heard, 'one day in the summer there was this battle and an English officer was killing

Turks all around him. He wasn't a very friendly type, but successful you know, even boasting. "Come on Johnny Turk" he shouted at a fellow who was attacking me.'

'Was it like a Munster Final', I asked.

'Not exactly,' he smiled. 'Anyway, the two lads were hopping around swinging their swords. They stopped and the Englishman said, "goodbye Johnny Turk", the Turk just smiled. "Shake your head", he said. The Englishman smirked and did so. His head, still smiling, fell off and rolled away.'

'His sword was sharp', I said.

'You could say that!' he said. 'Anyway, I made myself scarce and that's why we're going to the Munster Final tomorrow'.

My aunt was polishing the shoes, 'Go to bed child, and you ought to have more sense', she said to my uncle. We went to bed.

The little room below the kitchen was still warm from the heat of the day. I left the door ajar so that I could see the last embers on the fire glow and then grow cold as a pale moon threw its fretted shadow across the apple tree outside the kitchen window and on to the dresser near the big hanging clock which ticked and tocked and ticked and tocked. I had a small fear that the Holy Souls might have been disturbed by their mention in 'the trimmings' and been moved to come back but soon I drifted off into a restless sleep. My dreams were disturbed by the barking of Curtins' dogs and the ghostly screams of a vixen in Kelly's fairy fort.

The morning, as I knew it would, dawned grey and grew to bright and sunny. A milking roster for the weekend was arranged with a careful instruction to 'milk Crowley first as she gets a bit nervous if she's kept waiting'. She was called Crowley because she was bought from a man of that name. She was a great milker but a little bit fussy!

The little car was pushed out and then with the help of the starting handle, she protested into noisy life much to the annoyance of the hens who were about to eat their breakfast. My uncle kicked all the wheels on the car. My aunt put sandwiches and overcoats in the boot. I was given a dozen eggs for my mother and we were away.

Ger Ryan stopped us at the corner to wish us luck and told us, as if we didn't know, that, 'myself and Mrs Ryan will listen to all of ye on the wireless on Sunday'. I was delighted. I felt promoted to sharing the match with Michael O'Hehir.

Mrs Ryan shook the holy water saying 'may the Lord have mercy on the dead!'

Maurice said, 'she's praying for Tipp'. Wishful thinking. It would be my first Munster Final not listening to the wireless. Strange wasn't it! Every village in east Cork was smiling in the sun. They were all waiting like we were for tomorrow, red and white flags, home-made, hung on every gate and window. We took a break outside Fermoy on an afternoon full of promise where blackbird song and two noisy magpies seemed to foretell good fortune. My uncle drank a pint along the way and talked with great authority on Cloyne and Christy Ring.

We spent the Saturday night in my hometown in Charleville driving up and down the main street full of grandeur and waving to the 'lads' on Lyon's Corner. Charleville was agog because one of our own, John 'Danno' Mahony would be playing for Cork tomorrow. It was the real stuff of CJ Kickham's *Knocknagow*. My uncle had another pint in Davy Ryan's, told everyone that he was from the Cloyne area, not exactly true, and that he knew relations of the great Ring. He was quite annoyed when I chipped in to talk about 'our man' on the team. Still, the locals were impressed. Maurice said, 'for God's sake don't remind him of Johnny Turk!' I didn't! When we got back to 45 Holy Cross Place, my mother had kept the tea waiting but she joined in the general excitement and even added in three Hail Marys for Cork at the end of the Rosary trimmings.

Canon Burke's first Mass on Sunday was a spiritual and physical agony. The canon took forever and what with watch-watching and fervently exhorting St Jude to do the business and strike down the men of Tipperary, the Mass moved on leaden feet. The Canon's sermon, all 15 minutes seemed interminable. Anyway, as things turned out, God was certainly not a Corkman but I didn't know that at the time!

Departure time was ten o'clock – more holy water, good wishes, and we were part of a vast throng heading for the game. We arrived in Limerick in the best of good time. The car was parked carefully, pointing towards home with the handbrake in the ON position. With overcoats on, just in case, we walked down O'Connell Street, Limerick in sweltering heat.

I had never seen so many people in the one place, not even at the Charleville November Fair. It was rumoured that more than 42,000 people attended the match that day, never mind the thousands who were locked out. We were lucky.

After a cheap but eventful trip on a jaunting car pulled by a broken-winded pony we arrived near the Limerick Gaelic Grounds.

The atmosphere was inimitable and incomparable. The noise was living and vivid. All of Daniel Corkery's *Hidden Ireland* seemed to have converged on this place, where the music of every Munster accent cascaded on and on like the waves on Ballyshane strand on a summer's day. We were variously exhorted to buy, 'pears, bananas, oranges and chocolates – only the best', from a little woman by the roadside.

My Uncle Jim was suddenly galvanised into action. He saw a man from Whitegate, Co. Cork. They met and solemnly shook hands, delighted to meet so far away from home. I thought that I saw Mick Mackey but, of course, I wasn't sure. Br Ryan, a Clareman, thought that I had grown into a fine young man. He was always charitable. An elderly ballad-singer with his left hand clapped over his left ear, gave a plaintive rendering of 'Bould Robert Emmet' and it might have been the Dunne Brothers, friends of mine in a later life, who played a lively version of 'The Mason's Apron' and then succumbed to constant requests for 'The Banks' and 'Slievenamon'.

The crowd pressed inexorably towards the gates, Cork and Tipp all together in good humoured banter. I rushed up the sideline to see if I could find Michael O'Hehir. He was our only link with great hurling and, even if I couldn't, as usual, hear him, at least I might see him. I failed to do so and my day was all the poorer for it. The fact that this was one of the great Munster finals is immaterial. All that are left to me now are names, names that live deep in the heart and enrich my life with golden memories of a July day in Limerick when Christy Ring played the game of his life.

Tipperary won and, as we headed for Charleville, tears fell but our lives would never be the same again for greatness, tangible and overpowering, perhaps never to be seen again, was ours in the heart and, of course, there was Ring, the Cuchulainn of Cloyne of whom there would be more, much more, and very soon.

Ballyshane and The Summer Of Boyhood

Ballyshane itself is a townland close to the rocky coast west of Ballycotton Bay and east of Roche's Point, a coast at once cruel and beautiful, both graveyard and safe harbour to many ships and it was here that I spent the happiest summers of my youth.

Placenames and field names like An Poll Buí, An Croisairín (the little cross), Pairc a 'Bháire, The Devil's Elbow, the North Bog and the Pump Field remain fresh and clear after more than 60 years. The family farm was of the mixed variety and yielded an adequate living to my ancestors.

Charleville and Ballyshane are linked inextricably in my memories, one a sometimes winter and the other a perpetual summer of boyhood and early manhood. The former symbolised schooldays and work days while the latter has survived as a series of sun-flecked and sea-speckled summer memories. Ballyshane was my golden time when I was almost free.

The pavements of the Grand Parade in Cork City were festooned with travellers and messenger boys as CIE men called out names for destinations, some remote and familiar, like 'Whitegate, stopping at Carraigtwohill, Midleton and any other stops deemed necessary'. We hurried towards our vehicle and the conductor helped those who wished to put bicycles and baggage on the roof while the driver, Mr Paddy O'Connor waited until all his passengers were on board.

'All aboard, all aboard' and a journey to the sea had begun. All the buses seemed to leave simultaneously and we travelled down the South Mall with a tired and smoky hum. On our left, on the lower road was the famous Arcadia Ballroom across the road from the Railway Station from which emanated shrieks and puffs of smoke.

There was a stop in Carraigtwohill, famous for hurling and then down the long, prosperous main street of Midleton bearing right for Ballinacurra, passing on the way the convent where my mother went to school. By now my heart was pounding as the bus chuffed onwards towards Whitewell Cross where I said goodbye to the Whitegate bus and saw my cousins waiting in the pony and trap to bring me to journey's end.

My cousin's 'sit up now' signalled our first hill as everyone sat forward in the trap to make life easy for the climbing pony. Landmark after familiar landmark went by. Smells of summer and newly cut hay filled my nostrils. Cattle gazed lazily and disinterested behind gates. Dogs barked us onwards and from behind Curtins' gate, the grey and white gander stretched his neck in a silent hiss. And then, as if by magic I had my first look at the evening sea, which now without its glisten, rested blue and still to the far horizon. This was Ballyshane and, with a sharp turn right at the Croisairín, the pony, who seemed to know she was home trotted purposefully in the boreen, the middle of which was summer green and we were into the yard for the annual happy welcome.

This was a boyhood land where fact and fancy intermingled and where time seemed still and everything appeared to be as I had left it the year before.

This was a place where well-thumbed and well-loved books were once again touched and yet again read. The blue cover of *The Lights of Leaca Ban* faded and ragged, the bulky *Percy the Schoolboy Baronet,* a copy of *Blackcock's Feather* like the one I kept in Charleville and old editions of *Masterman Ready* and *Mr Midshipman Easy* sit silently side by side. I always brought *Flowers from Many Gardens* with me, an anthology of poetry published by the Christian Brothers and bearing on it to the present-day names of other owners, other times like 'James Lysaght, Main Street, Doneraile, Co. Cork', 'Harry O'Grady, Mallow Road, Doneraile', those of my two cousins Kitty and Maurice Duhig and of course my own name written and dated no fewer than eleven times from 12.9.1946 until 23rd October 1957 and a grand address which terminated on 'The World' and 'The Universe' – no crises of identity possible then. The foreword to *Flowers from Many Gardens* reminds me of what Hal Roach used to say 'write it down'. The advice is simple:

> In reading authors when you find
>
> Bright passages that strike your mind,
>
> And which, perhaps, you may have reason
>
> To think of at another season:
>
> Be not contented with the sight,
>
> But take them down in black and white;
>
> Such a respect is wisely shown,
>
> As makes another's sense his own.

The house was long, single-storeyed and thatched, its gable-end facing the road. The hall door, not often open, faced the garden. The back door, fronted by a portico, faced onto the farmyard. I say single-storeyed but there was a 'loft', approached by a narrow stairs, above the two small rooms below the kitchen. The kitchen was the domain of my two aunts, my cousin's mother, Maggie and her unmarried sister Jo, either of whom would trim the oil lamp on the wall near the only window in the room. I mention this only because soon after my epic day travelling and after tea, darkness began to drift in across the land and rest was invited to the crackle of sticks on the open fire and the murmur of Hail Marys in the nightly Rosary. My uncle Jim, my favourite person but not my real uncle, married to my aunt Maggie would soon leave the kitchen and retire to what I called the middleroom.

Beyond this and up a little hallway was the parlour, dark and unused, filled with the faded, desiccated opulence of a dark coloured chiffonier, a round table and a large sofa. Ancestors' photographs looked severely down on you and the new generation gazed a little fearfully up at them, skirting the dark heavy furniture and the fire only lit for breakfast for the parish priest at the 'station' mass. You went through this unlived place to the upper room where my Aunt Jo slept in spinster isolation.

Like I've said, a hallway linked the upper and lower ends of the house and here on a table in a glass case sat an ageless, stuffed pheasant while above him an old framed print showed a cavalry regiment from the British Army charging on to inevitable and timeless glory. The pheasant shook eerily every time you tapped his surrounding glass.

The garden was a haven where you hid under currant bushes and ate the produce! It was here long ago that my Aunt Jo first heard the banshee. 'She cried all the way into the garden from as far away as the Croisairín. She was like a woman in great sadness, her wail rising and falling and it all happened in the middle of the day. Our father died not long afterwards'.

It was in this house that many of my ancestors died, many of them long before their time, at a time indeed when consumption 'had no pity on blue eyes and golden hair'.

There were pictures there of a gentle-looking young man, my uncle Thomas, called 'Sonny', who died in his youth and who seemed to me to gaze wistfully towards a future that never was. Here too, was my grandmother, Catherine, dead long before her time and leaving her husband and young family desolate. She had however, gained a reprieve earlier on. My grandfather, Maurice, obviously beside himself with grief, sent for the local curate who came on horseback from Aghada to pray over her. As my mother once told me, he was thought to be a man of great spiritual powers and prayed for a long time. My grandmother's days were briefly extended but at a price. She recovered, but a valuable young colt died in the stables and, as she said, 'the Lord gave and the Lord took away'.

My mother, who was the youngest of all that Cashman family in Ballyshane, remembered too a barbaric and cruel custom, that of removing young children from the environs of the dying. When my grandmother subsequently died, her little family were removed to the cold yard in their night-clothes. Her journey from this life to the next was undisturbed. Then the clocks were stopped, the mirrors were covered. Time and place were out of joint.

There was a strange and grim story, too, of the death of my uncle Jamesy. He was buried with all due propriety in the family graveyard in Inch. As my mother told it, 'there was a custom that they, the spirits of the dead would come back to their home on the first Saturday night after their death'. Anyway, they were all saying the Rosary around the fire on the first Saturday night after our uncle's death when they heard the sound of horses and carriages coming into the yard. 'We were all silent, there was a step, the latch of the kitchen door was lifted, dropped and then the steps retreated and the carriages, or whatever they were, left and headed towards the Croisairín. No one said a word!' I'm not surprised and have no comment to make one way or the other. Be all this as it may, that house had its mysteries and could be a chilling place and I spent many a sleepless night listening to the ticking of the kitchen clock and my heart beating in time.

One experience I had, is related but yet removed from Ballyshane. It occurred when another of my aunts who had been a nurse in Dublin became ill at the beginning of 1946 and my father, not so well himself, went to Dublin. On the night before her death we were all, my sisters Kitty, Mary and myself in bed in my mother's room in Charleville. The Rosary was being said when I heard a most dreadful crying around the house which went on for a seemingly long time. My mother crossed herself and said 'your aunt is dead' and she was. Later on, nothing would persuade my mother that anything other than the banshee had come to warn us. That all happened in late February 1946 and I have never forgotten it. What was it? Who knows? 'There are more things in heaven and on earth ...'

It was not, however, all gloomy and sinister on my summer holidays in Ballyshane, especially not on the sports days when young men strove with might and main to win cycle races, donkey derbys, pillow fights and a long-distance run from Ballinrostig Church to the sports field. I saw one young man spit blood as he won while Cuck Maguire, a local character and noted reciter, stood on the ditch and without invitation incanted,

> Did they dare to slay Hugh O'Neill?

> Yes they slew with poison him they feared to meet with steel.

or when a neighbour of ours, Pad Garde wept openly as he recited with great vehemence 'The Drunkard's Dream'.

Here in east Cork, the sad and the glad commingled and my boyhood summers of the 1940s and 1950s were enriched. This was a time when children knew their place and where 'Mr' and 'Miss' described our betters and the old order seemed written in stone. This was accepted, but for the surprising subversions of my Aunt Jo who, while knowing her place, knew everyone else's as well. She warned me, 'never use the word Mr or Miss to one when you wouldn't use it to another'. Suffice to say that certain wealthy landowners were referred to by some as 'Mr Harry, Miss Maggie, Miss Marjorie', but never so by my aunt nor, indeed, by me!

This was the end of the era of the travelling man or the travelling woman. Never beggars, they walked the roads of east Cork from town to town, village to village and were generally welcomed wherever they went. I supposed they were like verbal newspapers bearing with them the local news from parish to parish. One such man was Gerry Mullane. The dogs didn't even bark when he came into the yard with news of cousins in Ballymacoda or haymaking in Churchtown South. He spent many a summer evening by the hob listening to Vincent Kelly telling stories or my Uncle Batt playing the accordion or the jew's harp. Night was spent in a shakedown in the barn and before he left after a hearty breakfast, he was urged to 'call again' and 'tell our cousins in Warren we were asking for them and the old sow produced a great litter'. Later, if and when any traveller became old and infirm they were visited in the local hospital and they were never buried without being remembered.

There were other callers too of a more worldly nature. These, like the 'Jewman', who was probably a Muslim, arrived in due season bearing with them ladies' cross-over aprons, straw hats, blouses, trousers, artificial flowers, statues of the Child of Prague, mouse-traps and other sundry supplies for farmers' wives. They were welcomed in a more businesslike way, laying their wares on the kitchen table or opening large suitcases on the kitchen floor. The exchanges were never impersonal and food was always offered and accepted. The odd garda often called eliciting no little suspicion because echoes of earlier times and earlier uniforms were not quite forgotten. Indeed, a long time earlier when my father was courting my mother, he cycled out in uniform from Cloyne to be greeted by the servant boy telling the woman of the house, 'Christ missus, there's a peeler outside'. No damage was done. Only now the gardai called socially or for business to do with tillage figures or the iniquitous warble fly. No problem. Everyone knew their own place.

Sunday Mass in Ballinrostig when we sat in the Cashman Family seat was much cherished by the older generation. They travelled in the pony and trap while we generally walked across the fields and on the roads, joining in with young Kellys and others on our way. The church boasted three aisles. We sat sideways to the altar in the seat our grandfather paid for while across from us sat the Kellys from Ballyshane in their seat. Miss Kelly, with chin on hand gazed haughtily across the altar. Mr Eugene, so known, wore a summer blazer and slacks, while Vincent who farmed the land and did not merit a 'Mister' wore his Sunday suit.

My Uncle Jim sat on the outside of his seat, looking spruce and clean-shaven although often bearing a little plaster on the cuts from his once-a-week shave. The priest was usually brisk and sharp in his sermon. I remember the odd Holy Hour, somnolent and warm after a summer day when the candles, the dusk and the sleepy crows were gentle accompaniments for incense, rosaries, blessings and hymns. These hymns are always in my mind, the 'O Salutaris', the 'Tantum Ergo' and above all else the closing hymn, 'Nearer my God to Thee' which they used to say was played by the band as the *Titanic* sank and the captain adjured those about to meet their maker to 'Die like British'.

The hymns were always led in style by Dan McCarthy, the organist who came from Aghada. His great baritone voice rang round the holiday church of my boyhood, eclipsing even the odd wheezing of the harmonium. Somewhat later in life, I listened every Sunday morning to a BBC radio programme called 'The Chapel in the Valley'. Their singer, with a voice like Dan's, was 'Mr Edwards'.

A great social and commercial event that lives on in my memory reflects long summer nights and early dawns driving cattle more than ten miles to the fair in Midleton. This was an occasion when cattle and youngsters were united in fear of the dark and in haste to get 'a good spot at the fair', we usually left Ballyshane at about 1.00 a.m. and I dreaded having to run along in front as, not alone was I on my own but I was a target for cranky sheepdogs and had to 'block' side roads from the cattle and then run on ahead. Midleton was a relief but standing around if you did not sell the cattle quickly was painful, no worse though than suffering the blandishments of 'tanglers' or 'jobbers' as they thrust advice, mostly insincere, at you, endless hand slappings and cautions of the 'don't break my word' calibre. A neighbour said of one such tangler, 'that's a man for you, he's as sincere as a whore's kiss.' Probably true. I didn't know what he meant.

Anyway there was always breakfast at Miss McSweeney's Emporium, a few shillings for lemonade and, if you were lucky, a lift home when your Uncle now cheerfully glowing might ask you to recite 'The Wreck of the Hesperus' or the more sentimental tale of the Ormonde peasant's daughter with 'Blue Eyes and Golden Hair'. Horror of horrors! Maybe you didn't sell and the long walk home into darkness was all before you with cattle as tired and as bored as yourself. Yes, indeed summertimes in Ballyshane were unforgettable and have never left me.

My University Days

My introduction to University College Cork was less than auspicious. Having arrived late for the matriculation exam, I had to beg for admittance. But in the end, I made it, succeeded in my exam, and joined the signing-on ritual, standing in long, chattering queues for the various disciplines and presenting money at the appropriate places. I was only spoken to once. 'Are you a hurler, footballer, athlete?' The answer was simple, 'no but I'm a singer'. Their reply was equally simple, 'carry on thank you'.

I signed on for Arts even though my past might have led towards dentistry, but cash, of which I had little or none, decided and that was that. For once penury was right!

These were lovely autumn days. Excitement and new hopes were in the air. The generosity of youth was all around me. My first acquaintances in corridor and quadrangle became my friends and Liz McEniry, Vera Jones, Michael Riordan, Charlie Corkery, and Frankie Hickey from Bandon would be part of my student life for a long time. Still the old days were not so easily forgotten. My former employer from Charleville had recommended me for part-time work to Gus Healy, whose dental laboratory was in Grand Parade. Gus, a fine and generous man, was only too willing to help and soon I was immersed in the familiar smells of wax and plaster and a little financial sufficiency stabilised my existence.

I had decided to study English because its literature seemed most accessible and because BG McCarthy, author of *The Whip Hand,* a play which gave me a definitely wrong impression of its author, was head of the department. *The Whip Hand* was a play, at once sympathetic to its characters and very distinctly in the 'kitchen sink' mode, suggesting to me that its author was perhaps in tune with the countryside and the characters that emerged from it. I was right and wrong simultaneously. Professor McCarthy – Brigid G, the writer, presented us with a different face in the lecture halls of UCC. I did not know it then but she represented and revealed a side of her personality far closer to her seminal work, now re-issued, *The Female Pen,* than to the simple, happy, one-dimensional world of *The Whip Hand*. It would take me a full university course to recognise a synthesis between seemingly disparate parts.

Then there was Irish, an easy decision, because all my life I had equated our native language with love of country and patriotism, believing that my boyhood reading of Pearse would be a valuable adjunct to my impending studies. How wrong I was.

European and Irish History seemed an obvious choice and Latin followed because I was misguidedly led to believe that it would make my academic life complete! English, Irish and History were undertaken as honours subjects and Latin limped in under the pass format.

That first term at University College Cork was as near to that overused word 'idyllic' as you could hope to find. Here was I, a nervous vulgarian at large, buying college scarves, ties and a new pair of shoes that would last me all through college. The time was here, plenty of it, to sample the doughnuts of the restaurant, coffee at threepence and to join College Societies. I am not much of a joiner unless I am in charge but I put my name down for An Chuallacht Ghaelach and attended one meeting before deciding that its fusty elitism was not for me.

The English Department under the leadership of the formidable and sometimes idiosyncratic leadership of Brigid G McCarthy was our introduction to the world of study and pressure. I remember well the first lecture. Gowned and notebooked, expectancy on every face, we sat. Professor McCarthy swept in. 'This is a class for pass and honours students', she declaimed. The word 'imperious' springs to mind. I sat next to Seamus Byrne from Castlemartyr and I remember he nudged me hard when she said, 'all Pass students stand please'. They did. 'Ah' she said, 'the poor we have always with us'.

The Irish class introduction was no less formidable. Risteard A Breatnach was our mentor and he seemed even less impressed with us than we were with him. Phrases about being 'intellectually committed' or indeed, otherwise were liberally sprinkled through his introduction. Anyway, for one reason or another he decided never to talk to us in the Irish language, so, for all our time in university we were addressed in English. It was the most discouraging and dispiriting aspect of university life. It was no wonder that the honours Irish classes were limited to a tiny number!

During my days in national and secondary school, we had studied Irish in the 'old' way with letters aspirated and an 'invented' form of writing, e.g. ƀ for b, ꝺ for d, ꝼ for f, etc., and without the dreaded 'h' to denote aspiration. So, my introduction to Irish literature, some middle and some modern and to forms of spelling, grammar and literature was quite foreign to me. The 'Roman' script was now the reality and, as I was older than everyone else in class, I was probably unique in being almost unable to read and certainly unable to spell and write it. However, I learned it and carried on as best I could.

There were, however, compensations in the Irish faculty. Seán O Tuama, then a young lecturer breathed a little life into our faltering system. It was he who had responsibility for the one hour of modern Irish in the week's schedule and his Saturday literature classes were highlights in my crowded week. The exciting discovery of ever expanding perimeters of Irish literature when modern writers like Seamus O Ceileachair, Liam O'Flaherty and others were explored with good humour and skill allied to the earlier work of the likes of Maire Bhuí Ní Laoghaire whose epic story of the fight at Ceim an Fhia, heroically simple in style, enriched my life. It would be years later when writing and presenting a television series from Bantry House that I met a descendant of one of the protagonists in Maire Bhuí's great poem. Later still, during one of my walks, the late great Seán O Síocháin regaled us with memories of his west Cork childhood and talked of the great regard for Maire Bhuí Ní Laoghaire. Many a night ended with his singing of Maire Bhuí's song – 'Cath Chéim an Fhiaidh'.

Incidentally, Sean O Tuama confirmed my own thesis that all good poetry is best read aloud and his classes bore dramatic witness to this. Another medium in our foray into the literary and spoken word was the poetry of Eibhlín Dhubh Ní Chonaill.

We read and said aloud her powerful poem 'Caoineadh Airt Uí Laoghaire' where the music of the words flowed over us and the accent and the sound of Munster certainly awoke in me a whole new composition of thinking and of feelings. Not a syllable was lost, not a note was dropped as we supped deep and long at the well of our culture.

These Saturday morning sessions, practising the spoken language and Seán's sharing of his deepest feelings with us, remain sharp and clear in my mind.

Caoineadh Airt Uí Laoghaire – The Lament for Arthur O'Leary, composed after his death by his widow Eibhlín Dhubh, was once described as 'the greatest poetry written in these islands in the eighteenth century'. It commemorates Art O Laoghaire, a Catholic, who was shot while on the run in 1773. Earlier he had refused to sell his fine horse for £5 (the maximum legal worth of a horse owned by a Catholic), after he had a race against Morris, the High Sheriff of Cork. Art is buried in Kilcrea Abbey, a few miles west of Cork City.

All the poetry and prose we learned from Seán O Tuama was spoken out loud and I can still hear his soft Cork 'blas' reciting the *Caoineadh* all of which I can recite with ease! The first verse is well worth remembering:

> Mo ghrá go daingean tú!
> Lá dá bhfeaca thú
> Ag ceann tí an mhargaidh
> Thug mo shúil aire dhuit
> Thug mo chroí, taithneamh duit
> D'éalaíos óm athair leat
> i bhfad ó bhaile leat.

A rough translation would run:

> My love you are forever!
> The day that I saw you
> At the gable of the market-house
> My eye took notice of you
> My heart gave joy for you
> I fled from my father with you
> Far away from home with you.

Before I leave Sean O Tuama I should say that the work of his friend Seán O Riordáin played a large part in our First Year lives. I played a small part in one of O Tuama's plays, *Ar Aghaidh Leat a Longadain*. I do not believe I had any speaking lines! When the run was over, Seán and his wife Betty invited us to a party in their house and I met the young O Tuamas for the first time.

It was an all-night affair and among the guests I remember Aindrias O Gallchoir and John O'Sullivan, two famous broadcasters from the Cork Studios of Radio Eireann. The sound of their voices rather than the content of their conversation remains in my mind. I remember being very impressed and wondering if ever I could reach such heights! Oh yes, we finished the very happy party by attending 6.00 a.m. Mass in Holy Trinity Church, across the road from where RTE Cork is now. Talk about future events casting shadows!

One day Seán asked us if we had ever made love through the medium! The silence was deafening. Only the nuns in the front seat were prepared to reply. He suggested that until passion, in word and act, was conveyed through our native tongue, we were seriously inadequate.

Breandan O Buachalla was demonstrator during my first year in College and I touched the eminence of 47.5 for my first essay. Cormac O Cuilleanain led us through the labyrinthine world of early modern Irish literature and his great sweeping chalk symbols across the blackboard were unforgettable, as was his constant cry, 'find your poet'.

The world of Irish history was in the capable and realistic hands of Professor Seamus Pender whose sardonic but kindly sallies prompted us through the eighteenth-century world of William Lecky and onto the sometimes more biased creation of *Ireland Under the Union*, by PS O'Hegarty. But for me the world of First Arts ignited through the often-lyrical and well-modulated tones of Kennedy F. Roche as with many a flick of his well-manicured fingers he conducted us through the French Revolution.

We were invited into and remained integral parts of his world. You might say that he ensured we were on intimate terms with Louis XVI and Marie-Antoinette, that we traversed the sea-green, incorruptible world of Robespierre, conducted ourselves in the world of Citizen Carnot and, in short were more at home with Monsieur Le Guillotine than we were in the world of 'Desiderius'. Kennedy would sit back in his chair and certainly transported me to the best of times and often the worst of times. I even read *A Tale of Two Cities* and was sometimes uncertain as to where Mr Roche began and where Mr Dickens ended. I look back with great affection on the lectures of Kennedy F. Roche, my ideal of what a university lecturer ought to be. Even if Napoleon's campaign seemed to be neglected and even if all I knew about him seemed to centre around his famous horse, 'Marengo' which we always believed was bought in Buttevant, there was no harm done!

I shall draw a veil over the Latin course under Messrs Treston and Fogarty – a very small veil, which would suffice to cover my own knowledge of the subject. Not I might say, any of their fault. Still I had one policy in First Arts, to avoid personal contact with the academic staff. To this I clung and having seen too many endeavouring to cross words with BG McCarthy, I know now that my decision was not just right but entirely necessary. Seán O Tuama was the only exception.

Spare time during First Arts was a limited commodity. Walking to and from Buxton Hill in Sunday's Well provided all the exercise I needed. Fitzgerald Park provided a museum and walks by the river as one looked up towards the opulent gardens of Sunday's Well. I crossed the suspension bridge every day and now and again attended soccer matches in the Mardyke. On Sundays, when returning home in the dusk was a poetic experience. Swans on the river and smoke curling up gently from every chimney allied to the smell of Sunday fries encouraged one to hurry home to tea and Radio Eireann for a sometime series with the Audrey

Park Ensemble, the Sunday night play, Gaelic Sports News with Seán O'Ceallachain or even attending *Othello* in the city with the great Anew McMaster in the leading role and from whom the great words glowed and flowered into the heart. One always remembers his anguished: 'then must you speak of one that loved wisely but too well' ... to almost coin a phrase, 'a fellow of infinite jest'.

Summer came and Mick Barry, the great Bowls player, cut the college grass and the anguish of exam time drew near. The examinations themselves, honours in English, Irish, History and pass in Latin were endured with many a vain regret for long mornings spent supping in the restaurant. By some amazing fluke I have the Latin papers from that summer. The questions are as turgid, as muddy now as they then were. The second paper has us translating Virgil from Latin to English. Question two is coy, 'scan the first two lines'. Later on we are asked to describe briefly the Battle of Trasimene. Oh dear, 'veni, vidi' and little else!

The results. Terror in the long corridor. Heat outside, in here the coolness of success or failure. Let's look, yes Denis you're there! One pleasing result – goodbye Latin. Tomorrow we leave, not to fresh woods but third class on the *Inisfallen* to Fishguard and then to Paddington Station in London. The only feeling was one of relief and exhaustion.

This was my first time on British soil, first ride on an escalator. Seamus Byrne, my companion in First Arts, and a young man called Rupert Swann were my companions. Seamus had arranged accommodation and employment for us in Aylesbury in Buckinghamshire. Travelling up by train we discovered a beautiful county and soon met up with Eileen Graham, a nurse from Killeagh in Co Cork who had made all the arrangements and brought us to our ultimate destination, the Stoke Mandeville Hospital where we were interviewed and without much difficulty were confirmed in summer jobs. We were soon to be ward orderlies. The lady said, 'not too difficult a job but you need a good strong back and stomach'. No problems there, or so I thought.

Accommodation was comfortable and I saw television (black and white) for the first time. At half past seven the following morning we were at action stations. We were the only English speaking orderlies. My first task was to shave a gentleman who was paralysed from the neck downwards. I was petrified but with his kindly help I managed the job. Then I discovered the enormity of our task. All of the patients, many of them veterans from World War Two were paralysed and it was our job to assist them every way we could. Seamus, Rupert and I met for coffee-break. There was no conversation. The courageous young men from UCC were found out but we decided to carry on.

The ward sister, who was a Scot, had a great eye for malingerers and I certainly fitted that category. After assisting at an inducement of bowel movement and having thrust off my gloves in the sluice, I decided that craft rather than courage or good-natured kindness was my metier. But the Scotswoman had met my kind before. 'Paddy' she said 'I have a permanent job for you, no more lurking in corridors, no more secret tea-making in the Rest Room, no more reading papers in the toilet, you are our new sluice officer and glove cleaner, get on with it'. I did and left soon afterwards. I think I lasted four days. My departure caused no ripple, cost the great hospital nothing and drew on me the fire of the irate matron. Seamus and Rupert also left and we parted ways. We were sadder, certainly poorer and definitely wiser than before.

'The Old Beams' was a restaurant in the Market Square in Aylesbury and it was here that I worked for the next two months. The proprietors were Mr and Mrs Hempsel, whose young daughter Avril often did her homework on the premises. The clientele was rural. The food was wholesome without being fancy, although there was great emphasis on properly set tables, especially on neatly folded serviettes, which word Mrs Hempsel preferred to napkins. I became a waiter and did very well on tips. I developed an extreme taste for Banbury cakes; they were I believe a local speciality and were delivered every day. Mrs Hempsel was a kindly soul, for whom I had a great regard although I often found the customers extremely trying and on such occasions, to ease my irritation, I would sing 'Kevin Barry' under my breath with special emphasis on 'another martyr, etc.'

The chef was not easily forgotten. His name was Ray and like most of his kind he operated from a short fuse, especially when the much dreaded 'coach parties' arrived. I would take orders for a quite disparate selection of meals but Ray's answer was mostly the same, 'bleedin coach parties, bleedin' Denis, it's bleedin' fresh plaice and chips, thirty-six, the same for everyone'. They dined sumptuously on the best fish and chips I have ever tasted. One day the kitchen was even more fraught than usual; it seems a supplier was unhappy with some delay in payment and he took a cleaver to Mr Hempsel. Ray and I retreated but there was ultimately no harm done.

George was a splendid head waiter who taught me never to react to a customer's wagging finger. 'Remember my boy,' he said, 'the only dogs here are customers so never answer to finger clicking or whistling'. I didn't and it was a great summer.

Margaret was an English waitress and Annie, who was Irish, was my favourite. The customer whom I remember best was a friendly policeman. They made my stay in Aylesbury a very happy one in the far-off summer of 1958. Then in late 1997 I received a letter from Aylesbury to *Fáilte Isteach* and 39 years were bridged on the airwaves. A miracle for another time.

Back at UCC it was English and Irish, back to BG McCarthy, Riobaird Breathnach and Anglo-Saxon, May Conroy and a gentle trip through Chaucer's *Canterbury Tales*, and Seamus Caomhanach and Old Irish. There was, too, a life beyond academia. I played a small part in *The Beggars Opera* which was a great success in College.

The summer house examinations were tackled and overcome and through the kindness of Jack O'Connor, the accountant, I became the brand new night porter at the Southern Lake Hotel in Waterville. I brought with me a copy of the poems of TS Eliot and those of Gerard Manley Hopkins; both of these I found almost impossible to grasp and woke up one morning to find that I had torn a page of Eliot in a frenzied dream. 'The Waste Land' was proving elusive but still I tore up the page where Eliot summed it up for me then, if not now.

> Here is a place of disaffection
> Time before a time after
> In a dim light.

Still the month of June in that warm summer of 1958 remains among the most memorable of my life. Night portering with its polishing of shoes, room service and furnace-stoking as the dawn broke pink and beautiful over Lough Currane remains forever with me. The late Mrs Meldon was formidably and kindly in charge. The staff were warm, witty and with a healthy streak of Kerry cynicism towards life and time. I remember a room service call for tea and toast at 3.00 a.m. and my somewhat shocked realisation that both my customers were casually starkers! I nearly choked on my lobster which I usually ate before breakfast and going to bed. The staff dined as richly as the guests.

The smell of summer roadside flowers invaded my senses as I cycled most afternoons to spend some time with Seán O Donghaile (Johnny Donnelly) who talked Irish with me and told stories of Eoghan Rua and Aogán O Rathaille. The shock of hearing Irish spoken where it belonged and by one who had it from the cradle was intense and beautiful. I felt that I had come very close to my Kerry patrimony, closer that I would ever come again, or so I thought.

The downside, I learned at the end of June, was that £4 per week was insufficient to raise enough money for next year's fees, so it was farewell to the Kingdom, slán to Johnny, 'fear go raibh gaoluinn aige o dhuchas,' and to the luminous Kerry dawns of an almost lost time, I would never see its kind again but this tiny paragraph in the story of my life remains immutable. Goodbye to all the wild and beautiful Kerry nights and all the wild and beautiful people who made them so.

So from one lost innocence to another. It's evening time on Clapham Common in London with little money and nowhere to go. There are some three or four pucking a sliotar around. I introduce myself and explain my situation. They are sympathetic and invite me home to their apartment, where I stay free and grateful until I find my feet and a new summer career as a sandwich maker and grill hand at Fortes, 75 The Strand. I had an apartment, one room, in Baron's Court and from here I faced the heatwave and a summer of hard work and no little fulfilment and excitement. I wonder what became of the hurlers of Clapham Common. Where are they now?

The heat struck early in the London summer and the swell of customers swept through our little piles of fresh sandwiches as Martha, a little lady from Vienna, sat in her kiosk outside the door and craved the odd coffee which I brought her with pleasure even if only to hear her talk and her tales of her native city and her memories of Richard Tauber's concerts. The staff were somewhat more cosmopolitan than those of Waterville! Some came from the West Indies, there was a scattering of Italians, a few Irish and of course the Cockneys whom I liked best. I worked from 8.00 a.m. until 4.00 p.m. then took a break and worked in a downstairs grill until 11.00 p.m. when I took the tube from Charing Cross and back to Baron's Court.

The heat was intense and keeping down weight was no problem. The lovely street where I worked was a constant source of excitement; almost across the road *Salad Days* was playing while further up *A Raisin in the Sun* could be seen. We had many theatre people for snacks and this was how I met John Sleator, the stage and film actor. He invited me to tea in the Savoy (for which I wore the only suit I had) and a box in the theatre for *Ring of Truth* in which he was playing with David Tomlinson and Irene Browne. That was one of the great days.

One weekend was taken off and was a veritable blitzkrieg of culture and entertainment. I began with the matinée of *My Fair Lady* on the fantastic stage of Drury Lane. Alec Clunes, whose son Martin is now famous, played Professor Higgins and the production also featured Robert Coote and the inimitable Stanley Holloway. It was fantastic and cost five shillings in the gods. After tea I headed for the Queen's Theatre in

Shaftesbury Avenue and there Michael Redgrave and Flora Robson brought life and subtlety to *The Aspern Papers* by the already subtle and dark Henry James. I should have added that I had my lunch in the Embankment Gardens where much was provided by the colourful band of the Welsh Guards who played a Percy French medley which included 'The Mountains of Mourne'. I felt proud to be Irish and sang quietly with them, 'I met him last week I was crossing the Strand'.

Anyway to continue, on the Sunday I took the Tube to Holland Park for an open-air production of *A Midsummer Night's Dream*. It rained all day. There was no performance but later when the heat came back I met Bob Hope and Audrey Hepburn on Shaftsbury Avenue and got their autographs! I am not sure when but I know that around this time I also attended a 'Prom' with the BBC Symphony Orchestra in the Royal Albert Hall. They played the music of John Ireland and I pretended an interest! Lovely place though!

One Sunday morning I saw President Eisenhower being driven down the Strand as I grew more exhausted from my summer labours. I should say too, that I spent much of my spare time rambling around Soho, not so much sampling the fleshpots as just looking, although I, once or twice, went in. Nothing to write home about although there is a postscript. When I went to confession in St Augustine's Church in Cork, the priest was noisily unimpressed by my innocent tale of 'looking but not touching'. He suggested 'The Stations of the Cross three times' before you leave this Church'. I demurred. His parting shot left neither me nor those around the church in any doubt, 'young man', he said, 'you're the making of a blackguard' as he slammed the slide in my face. I left, quite disturbed. Outside in the street I remembered the name of a priest in St Mary's Pope's Quay who was kind to students. I galloped across and saw that he was 'hearing'.

'How long my child since your last confession?' he casually asked.

'Ten minutes', I said. There was a pause and he asked where I had been.

'Did you have absolution?' he asked.

'Sort of', I replied and told my story. He gave me a blessing and we said a civilized, 'good evening'. Thanks Fr Moran!

My last days in London were spent in visiting bookshops and in buying a second-hand briefcase in the British Rail Lost Property Office in the Strand. My financial affairs were well in order as Mr Tesler, the manager, had kept my money in the safe and apart from offering me full-time employment with Fortes, ensured that my hard-earned money was safe!

Third year in college was for work undiminished except for a production of *The Conspirators* by Schubert. Why this was chosen I'll never know but at least it seemed to please Professor Fleischman who came every night. Talking of productions and not strictly within the third year framework we presented *The Beautiful People* by William Saroyan in which I played an Irish parish priest much given to drink. Good casting! I was lucky not to receive a best supporting actor award at the Limerick Drama Festival. Hilton Edwards, who was adjudicator, confused my pauses from forgetfulness with artistic lulls in my performance. He was most impressed! So much for the individual talent of the artist.

I never remember not working that long year and every day I walked ten miles to and from college from the heights of Summerhill where I now lived. I bought a new pair of shoes and had dry feet. Long weekends were spent learning and the Whit weekend was spent locked in John Milton's *Paradise Lost* and *Paradise Regained*. I felt isolated, stowed away in my tower of study and loneliness.

The beginning of Canto Three best summed up my feelings at the time;

> But cloud instead, and ever-during dark
> Surrounds me, from the cheerful ways of men
> Cut off, and for the book of knowledge fair
> Presented with a universal blank.

I couldn't put it better myself.

The college friends retreated too into their working recesses and not even Jane Austen's *Emma* and the gregarious Miss Bates could cheer me up. I was reading seven Shakespearean plays almost simultaneously and TS Eliot's *The Wasteland* became bedside reading. My Irish studies were a constant grind without pleasure or enjoyment. The summer came, the grass was cut and there was no redress – our examinations were autumnal. By the time they came around I was certainly exhausted, hopeless and nearly moneyless. I was also constantly hungry.

The examinations themselves were quite predictable. All the hard work, all the learning was worthwhile. I would at least survive. There was one major catch, the 'compulsory question' in English Literature. After all the study I was unable even to attempt it. This was 'go for it' time. Instead of the 'compulsory' question I announced my intention of discussing the work of TS Eliot and his role in my life. I dredged up every word that I had ever read, and in particular based my answer on my long unrequested dissertation in Gilbert Murry's 'The Classical Tradition' and really went for it.

You see, I had learned all the poem and many of the critiques and especially this by Murry:

> There is not a phrase, there is hardly a word, which is not made deeper in
> meaning and richer in fragrance by the echoes it awakens ....

I proceeded to do likewise. I came out exalted and studiously avoided discussing the paper with my friends. My long walks in London, never alone but in poet's and people's company surged to my aid and memory and desperation combined and time and Eliot did the rest.

> A crowd flowed over London Bridge, so many
> I had not thought death had undone so many

All of which dropped delicately into my once-daily journey from Charing Cross Underground Station to my work-place in the Strand:

> This music crept by me upon the waters
> And along the Strand, up Queen Victoria Street . . .

All leading as Eliot might have said to

> The awful daring of a moment's surrender
> which an age of prudence can never retract.

BG McCarthy much later remarked that, as Arnold Bennett wrote of Eliot, I was 'sometimes walking near the limits of coherency,' perhaps, even, as Eliot might have said in another context, pursuing an 'illusion of being disillusioned.'

Once I acquired my degree, future plans were vital. I did not contemplate teaching, from a strange notion that my new journey in life would take me somewhere else. So it was that one day in October 1959, having already written for an appointment, I knocked on the door of Prof. BG McCarthy's house in 19 Wilton Road in Cork. A Masters Degree was my objective and before long and after the initial sparring in which she wondered why she had never been aware of me during my undergraduate days, she agreed to take me under her wing.

I had no choice in my subject. Almost without preamble she said, 'I think a writer from your own north Cork would be suitable and I think Elizabeth Bowen is the one. Would you like that as a topic?' I was struck dumb. I had never even heard of her. But like many another time in my life I judged the wind and mixing my surprised metaphors went with the flow! 'I suggest you read *The Death of the Heart* and some of her short stories and then come back to me. And now it's time for tea, you haven't met my aunt, have you?' Before I could reply the kind and gentle old lady entered with a tray and conversation became general. I learned that it might be a good idea to join the English Literature Society, which I subsequently did and became auditor for three great years. We had fortnightly readings and ranged far and wide from Chekhov to Shaw to Sartre to Donagh McDonagh to O'Casey to Joyce to Synge and so on. BG generally read the narration or female lead and I, thinking and knowing that all my birthdays had come together, produced and read the male leads. It was a happy if enclosed coterie who met in the Ladies Club or in BG's house for tea and readings.

Meanwhile I 'attacked' the Bowen subject, which I found sometimes dry, often intellectually taxing but always a great challenge. I discovered that she was born in Dublin but of north Cork stock, from the parish of Kildorrery in the townland of Bowen's Court only a few miles from Doneraile.

While all this was going on, I found myself part-time work teaching with my old confreres in Presentation College on the Western Road in Cork. Br Angelo was the superior and I was paid £4 per week, half the wages I had in my later days in Charleville but, like Mr Micawber, I felt sure that better times were ahead. I was warmly welcomed by the other teachers, such as Dan Donovan, a fine actor and soon to become a friend, Freddie Holland, maths teacher extraordinaire, Johnny Dorgan, Sean McCarthy and others whose names elude me now. As for the boys, well they were boys, some who cared, others who didn't although they all seemed cosseted. Little stands out in the month I spent there except I 'took' first years for rugby on the half-day. I carried a little green book of rules but always led from the back in an alien world!

One day, trawling for news on the notice board at University College, I saw that Henry Ford & Son Ltd. Cork intended employing a graduate trainee. Why not me? Before long I had arranged an interview with Tommy Brennan, managing director at Fords and shortly afterwards I was informed that I would be employed on a temporary basis by Fords for a salary of £10 per week. So, already I had more than doubled my teacher's wages.

On the weekend before I began my Ford experience, the English Literature Society embarked on an outing to 'Literary North Cork'. We set off in several motor-cars for Doneraile and when we arrived I suggested lunch in the grounds of Doneraile Court. It was a wild day and much to Prof. McCarthy's annoyance, Mrs Conroy failed to light the Primus and instead of tea, we dined on bottles of lemonade and sandwiches. Not a great start and worse was to follow.

We travelled towards Edmund Spenser's Castle and there by the roadside I met the late Lizzie Roche. I gave a little talk to our band of followers and turning to Lizzie rather grandly said 'This road leading by the poet Spenser's home has seen many stirring events and not a few have travelled on it on the way to our great literary past'.

Lizzie paused, looked me straight in the eye and realistically and kindly said: 'tis, tis indeed Sir, this is surely a busy road, especially on Sunday nights when the world seems on it, on the way to the Bingo in Charleville'. And it was!

The Years Of Our Ford

My years with Fords from 1961 to early 1964 remain clear. Jim Butler, who was Company Secretary, invited me into his office which sat at the centre of a great organisational web. When you entered there you waited until he looked up, stopped writing or were spoken to and you entered there by invitation. I had never been addressed by my surname before and must say that I disliked it. Anyway, it was decided that I should visit each department in the organisation in turn and report back to him after each foray. I remember that I enthusiastically began my notes 'This is a far better thing that I do than I have ever done'.

The Ford Motor Company in Cork, with a direct and personal link to Fords in Dearborn, Michigan through an old family connection in Ballinascarthy, Co. Cork was a busy and complex place. To be employed there was for many a place of haven and certainties where if you worked hard, did what you were told and respected your 'betters', you had a 'sound' job for life. There were no trade unions when I began. At knocking-off time each evening from Fords and Dunlops, the prosperity of Cork poured out the gates onto the crowded quays. Yes indeed, Henry Ford and his assembly lines gave back to Cork much more than his ancestors had taken with them from Ballinascarthy.

Paudie Sheehy, the Kerry footballer, and his assistant Finbar Ambrose were my mentors. They were in the Internal Audit Department and from there I roamed far and wide in my pursuit of information. I was generally well-received although I know that some felt I was probably a 'management plant'. Not true. The offices faced out onto the riverside and across the Lee up to the sylvan heights of Montenotte. In those early autumn days I loved watching the ships from Dagenham berthing at the quayside and unloading car parts securely held in large wooden containers. These same cases were known far and wide as 'Ford Boxes' and could be bought very cheaply for use as hen houses or dog kennels!

It was my first time too, to see men 'clocking in' although I have never had to do this. I was not just an employee, I was 'management'. Small birds were fed during lunch-time breaks although they were often at risk from vehicle 'hub caps' glinting in the autumn sun. The little birds were attracted to their reflections on them and then repelled and attacked their own images with fury. The result was often death.

My journeys about the offices and factory brought me to some wonderful people like Paddy Fox Collins and Josie Hartnett the two great hurlers from Glen Rovers, and Cork, Paddy McLoughlin, a mild mannered Dublin man whose hobbies were walking and literature and who initially always referred to me as 'Mister'! Then there was a small wiry and fiery man from Sunday's Well named Teddy Hanley. He had been a clerk in Ford's on the very first day along with Sir Patrick Hennessy, the 'main man' in Dagenham to which Cork was affiliated.

The 'girls', apart from secretaries like my friend Mary Barry from Banteer, were corralled without fences into the comptometer area and controlled calculating machines. I suspect that the regulations were as rigid as those for women students at university. No low-cut dresses, and certainly no bare legs! Going from post to pillar brought one up close to the rivalries, intrigues and gossip of a large organisation, no different, indeed from my experience later in RTE. I must say, however, that kindness and humour abounded.

When I had completed my course, the time had come for me to visit Dagenham where I would join a class of 'graduate trainees' from all over the world. I flew from Dublin. I was met on my first morning by the training executive whose first question was a surprise. 'Where do you dine in Cork, Executive I suppose?' Remember what I said about going with the flow! The answer was 'yes'. I should have told you that Cork had a rigidly stratified dining system. It ranged from factory canteen to senior executive dining rooms. I now found myself in this latter category and to celebrate this occasion, I grew a nice paunch which has never left me!

During my stay in England I was in digs with Mrs Rolfe in Collier Row, Romford. Food was also high on her priorities and I fed well on 'hearty' English breakfasts and dinners awash with sauces, puddings and beef and gravy. My evenings were spent watching television including the early days of 'Coronation Street', 'Emergency Ward Ten' and many others. I gained nearly two stones during my Dagenham days.

The romance of the motor-trade and pride in the shiny assembled vehicles was all around me. It was fantastic to see car after finished car drop off the line and then be driven away for testing. In fact, I bought my first car, a lovely two-tone turquoise and black 105E Anglia and followed her progress along the line. 'Bliss was it in that dawn to be alive'.

I had now joined the purchasing department and among my tasks was to assist with the annual audit of steel which took place every year at 'Springs Ltd' in Wexford.

This was a major event in the life of the department and Tom O'Keefe who was assistant purchasing manager who often bought curtains and other household requisites for the managing director's family, invited me to join him. He made it sound like getting an All-Ireland Medal! We would be accompanied by an 'operative' whose job it would be to actually spot-check and count the bars of steel.

So it was that Mr O'Keefe, Mr Dowling and Marcus Hurley set out in a 'company car' for Wexford. We dispensed with collar and tie for the journey. These were *de rigeur* for the office. The first culture shock occurred when we crossed Dunkettle Bridge. Tom, who was driving, said casually, 'by the way, Denis and Marcus, you can call me Tom from now on during our journey'. Marcus just said, 'Jesus' and I kept my peace.

We stayed in the Talbot Hotel in Wexford and Marcus settled into a guest house. I learned Tom's life story, how he played tennis at home in Cobh even wearing 'whites' at weekends, which reminded me of my reasons for not playing weekend tennis in Charleville. I tried my best to probe for information concerning the 'Executive Toilet' in Fords. Was it true there was a golden key? Tom, himself, had heard the story of a certain Ford executive who had publicly confused Elizabeth Bowen's name with that of my professor and never lived it down.

This particular gentleman had pretensions to grandeur and, while he worked in the personnel department, had the manners and approach of a bulldog. If he felt that you were his junior, well, his attitude was positively colonial. It is said that he once told startled colleagues in the executive dining-room that he 'knew personally Dowling's Professor whose name was Bowen!' I heard afterwards that he may have taken early retirement.

Towards the end of the week, Marcus broached a certain delicate matter. 'I always provide a little service to Mister ... sorry ... Tom on these trips?' I was intrigued but was quickly disabused of any sordid or lurid imaginings. 'I give him a free hair cut. Would you like one too?' Tom looked uncomfortable until I said, 'of course', and the following night, 'after hours of course', as Tom put it, we were given short back and sides. As he cut our hair Marcus confided, 'I could do lots of hair at the plant, it's like a little business really, they all come to me'. He proceeded to tell me where to go, even suggesting, 'you'd be in good company, I've cut the best of them, even in company time'. Tom sliced him with a look. Ever afterwards when I saw men emerging brushing their shoulders I knew that Marcus was on the job.

As we drove back to Cork, Tom and I restored our collars and ties and Marcus hid his clippers in his pocket. My days with Fords were brightened by the arrival of two other graduates, Donal Farmer, who later became very famous as the priest in *Glenroe* on RTE TV, and was also a distinguished Head of Drama in RTE and is known far and wide as a fine actor and producer; Enda Hogan who later on rose to the top in the Irish Permanent Building Society and was, as a former colleague once remarked to me, 'the third member of an unholy trinity from UCC which descended on Fords.' I am not exactly sure what he meant, but Messrs O Dulaing, Farmer and Hogan are as well-remembered as the Model T – well almost! Work on the thesis proceeded apace. Mary Murphy from Fords typed it and BG McCarthy with large slashes of blue pencil consigned it to 'good for Pass but you have more in you'. I thanked her for shaping my life in her acerbic and realistic way. I owe much to her and acknowledge it here.

As for Fords, those days are never forgotten. It was, in many ways, a strange oasis in my life and the friends I made there are always with me. Their good humour and forbearance were exemplary. I am pleased to have shared in a unique slice of Cork life before it went away. I was part of what Huxley might have called 'The Years of our Ford'.

Memories remain, even if relationships have been severed by time and separation. Now and then I meet old colleagues and stories and names from the past are remembered. Maybe I only remember the good days but I have never forgotten the advice of Marcus, the barber of Fords, 'Remember one thing Boy, remember it well. When the boss smells gas, we all smells gas.'

The year 1961 was a most significant one for me. On St Valentine's Day, Tuesday, 14 February, Vera Galvin and I were married at 11 o'clock in the morning in the Collegiate Chapel of St Finbarr (the Honan Chapel) in University College, Cork. Not alone did that Tuesday fall on St Valentine's Day, but it was also Shrove Tuesday, the last day for marrying before lent.

Fords were agreeable to according me a week's holiday with salary while Vera's employers, the Department of Education accorded her one week as per regulations! I was not long enough at Fords for a 'going away' party or any other celebration but Jim Butler, the Company Secretary, asked if I 'needed a little advance'. Whether I did or not, I decided to leave well alone but I have always been grateful for the offer.

At this time, I lived in digs with Mrs Keane in Summerhill while Vera lived across the city on the patrician heights of Sunday's Well. Meeting and courting required ingenuity and shoe leather and I became a regular patron of the No. 14 single-decker bus to Sunday's Well. I generally caught the last bus at night from there to Patrick Street and, if or when I missed it, Dan Hoare, who was then courting his future wife Mary also in Sunday's Well would pick me up at my bus-stop near Buxton Hill and drop me into town on his beloved BSA motor bike. Before we went our separate ways, we usually drank a pint of milk and enjoyed a bun in an all-night cafe in Parnell Square.

On the night before my wedding, I travelled down by bus, carrying with me a large parcel containing my wedding clothes. Johnny, the bus conductor, who knew me well from my constant journeys in his bus sat alongside me on the long 'side seat'. When I was leaving he shook my hand and wished me a happy day tomorrow'. He stuffed a ten shilling note into my breast-pocket and I had tears in my eyes. He was normally a somewhat irascible and taciturn man which made his kind gesture all the more extraordinary. Life is enriched by such little acts of generosity.

Vera and I had organised the wedding like a military operation. My best man Cathal O'Corcora and groomsman Michael Riordan travelled with me to the church while Vera was accompanied by her two bridesmaids, my sisters Kitty and Mary.

Vera Jones, a dear friend from Croom in Co. Limerick, was the organist and Denis Leahy, a fine tenor from Kanturk was soloist. Fr Dan O'Callaghan, a curate in Aghada was celebrant assisted by Fr Andrew Barry of my Doneraile days and An tAthair Tadhg O Murchú, S.P., Carraig na bhFear. The entire ceremony, which went off without a hitch, was conducted in Latin, incidentally Frankie Hickey from Bandon took care of the tall hats for the Groom's Party!

Liam Kennedy took the pictures on the cold morning as 'Mr and Mrs Dowling' emerged from the dim and beautiful church. We were transported in style by limousine to the Metropole Hotel for the wedding breakfast. Food and speeches were perfectly in accord and by mid-afternoon we were ensconced in third-class splendour in the Dublin train at Kent Station. Cork had no airport at the time and we had decided to fly from Dublin to Paris.

The old Jurys Hotel in College Green was our immediate destination and later that evening, we walked down to the Savoy Cinema for tea. We chose the Savoy, because it reminded us of the same cinema in Cork and, I suppose because the food was familiar and reasonable!

Our first flight was via Aer Lingus on the following morning and we spent a great week in the Hotel Phénix near the Étoile in Paris. We went everywhere on foot and constantly dined sumptuously on rolls and black coffee. Paris was in its beautiful budding spring garb and entirely memorable.

We returned to our new apartment in Cork to discover that our bed had not yet been delivered. We slept well on the floor on the first night home and were thankful to two nun-friends from UCC who had delivered food to the flat during our absence. What did Wordsworth say of 'acts of kindness and of love'? Anyway, he knew what he was talking about!

* * *

My days with the motor-trade have spread a warm glow over much of my life. Harmony, success, friendship and peace were, for once, united within me. By a strange coincidence, that same motor trade has thrown me a few happy lifelines over the years. I am reminded of happy days spent with Tom and Kathleen O'Neill in their 1907 'Harvester' car and their leading me down a few fruitful byways of my life. One stands out: a lunch with Don Hall, peerless among the public relations fraternity and Eddie Thornton, general sales manager of the burgeoning Skoda organisation in Ireland.

Eddie regaled me with tales of his early days in the motor trade and his life among the 'Beetles', a life which ran parallel with my own in Ford and re-introduced me to the motor world. Tall tales and small tales coalesced and before I knew it I was invited to join a group of motoring journalists on a trip to Prague in the Czech Republic. We visited the Skoda headquarters and later that day I was thrilled to be brought to the shrine of the Infant of Prague. The peace and calm of that church cast a gentle benison on me and my fellow-journalistic travellers.

Far away from Ireland, in this beautiful city by the Danube, I was reminded of a rainy day near Lanesborough on the Shannon when I visited the home of the McGrath family. They were planning a picnic on the river bank to celebrate a holiday visit of many of their American cousins. Mrs McGrath was fearful for 'a wet day'. Not unreasonably, she found a solution. 'Twill be dry,' she said, 'We'll put the infant [of Prague] out in the hedge the night before. He'll take care of it.' We broadcast 'live' on the day and it was fine for the event. Mrs McGrath has since gone to visit 'the Infant'. He must have been pleased to hear of the great affection of the Irish, one of the few royals entirely acceptable here!

Prague was memorable and Eddie Thornton shared all my enthusiasms. His untimely death earlier this year robbed me of his kindly presence and compassionate and generous friendship. Suffice it to say, he was almost like the brother I never had.

Bob O'Callaghan, when speaking of the recent visit of the 'Tall Ships' to Dublin best summed up our friend's departure. 'He was', he said, 'called ashore before his time.'

There must be something special about 'motor' people. Their aura spans the decades. Names from my past continue to hail me from space and time. Paddy McLoughlin and Jack O'Brien meet across the car bonnets of eternity and modernity with the likes of Colin Sheridan and Larry Mooney. Aldous Huxley's 'year of our Ford' is like a recurring friendly decimal!

RTE – The Cork Story

After more than three years as a graduate trainee with Henry Ford & Son Ltd, in Cork I began to feel an urge to depart. I could see the results of my hard-won degree receding into the distance and my possibilities for preferment in the world of industry shrinking towards a mundane level. Somehow working in the purchasing department at Fords, where my main tasks seemed to centre around the ordering of nuts and bolts and filling of purchase order forms did not seem to be where my future lay. Then one day out of the blue, my colleague Tom O'Donohue, probably wiser than me, read an advertisement in the *Cork Examiner*. It concerned an opportunity on the staff of RTE, Union Quay, Cork. They required a Programme Assistant, whose duties would include broadcasting in Irish and in English and co-operating in every way with the Regional Officer. Tom said, 'try it anyway. It would suit you better than counting pounds of steel or looking out the window at the River Lee'. I wrote to RTE, listing all the achievements I could think of, and hoped for the best. To my surprise I received an application form, which I completed and sat back and waited. I had little enough hope but a burning desire to make my way into the arts world. I had no contacts, did not know anyone in RTE and, certainly had no pull. 1964 began with a cool invitation to attend for interview at the studios in Union Quay, Cork. I was in the hunt and instantly set about preparing myself for the ordeal.

I bought a Grundig tape machine and began practising talking into it. Hearing my own flat North Cork accent was a shock and did not compare well with the cultured tones I heard on the radio. I began to seriously listen! My hopes took a severe buffeting when I met a graduate colleague from my UCC days. He was full of news, 'I've just answered an advertisement for the radio in Cork. I think I have a great chance. I know two people who work in there and they think that I am a dead cert.' I said nothing. There was really nothing to say. And then, out of the blue, I was invited to present myself for interview at the Radio Centre in Union Quay. The invitation was signed by Síle Ní Bhriain, Regional Officer. I climbed the stairs for the very first time, casually carrying a copy of Oscar Wilde's Works which I bought that day. It brought me comfort. The man seated at the desk asked me to sit down and wait for 'herself to invite you in'. I sat and waited and a tall gaunt lady of striking appearance and wearing tweeds invited me into her office. She introduced herself as Síle Ní Bhriain. The office seemed all white and black. She invited me to be seated and introduced her two colleagues, Mr Kevin Roche and Mr Gerry McLoughlin. They remained relatively silent as she conducted the interview. The questions came with speed and courtesy. My past career was probed and analysed. Was not the Ford Motor Company a strange choice after a high-powered arts degree? Síle was much impressed by a laudatory letter from Professor BG McCarthy, Professor of English in UCC in which my efforts and achievements were presented in glowing terms. Questions arose concerning the Irish language. Did I speak it on a regular basis? Would I be capable of conducting broadcasts in it? Gerry McLoughlin dealt with Fords. Why did I wish to join RTE? Where did I see my future?

Kevin Roche threw in a question concerning orchestral scores. My somewhat tentative reply was inaccurate. I was severely under pressure. There were pauses. The interview board seemed a little constrained themselves. I knew that it was all to play for, and went for it, Síle dropped in a seemingly simple 'what is your favourite programme?' My reply was as inadequate as my emotions. 'There are many'. For what seemed an age the conversation was conducted in Irish and then, quite quickly, the interview was terminated and I was very unsure of myself. I was thanked for coming along. My hand was shaken and I was ushered out into the reception area. The man at the desk looked up and said, 'you were longer than all the others, good luck to you'. I got back to my car in a lather of sweaty unsuccess. Well, at least I had tried. About a week later, the phone rang in Fords. It was Síle Ní Bhriain. She informed me that I had been successful in my interview. I was speechless. She added, however, that I would have to undergo a microphone test, which was vital in confirming my position. I thanked her as best I could and confirmed that I could attend the studios on the following Saturday. The RTE studios seemed less strange now. The man at reception, whose name was Paddy O'Keefe, gave me some tea while I waited to be called for my audition. Oliver O'Brien, who was the technician in charge brought me down to the studio suite where I met Douglas Gunne who was balance and control officer. Síle materialised carrying a script which dealt with a walking holiday in Greece.

Without preamble I was ushered into a tiny talks studio with table, chairs and a hanging microphone. 'When you see the red light, you're on', she said, 'that is of course when Mr Gunne has adjusted the microphone to suit your voice and Mr O'Brien will then tape the material. Then as she left, she turned and said kindly, 'good luck'. The reading took about ten minutes and was a matter of gulps, poor phrasing and non-pronunciation of Greek place names. She sat in the control room with the technician and then her voice penetrated my headphones, 'thank you Mr Dowling, that will do for now. Would you care to join me in my office'. I did and was rapidly discovering that 'Mister' was the order of the day. 'I listened to the tape', she said. 'You did very well, but why did you never say the place names?'

I paused. 'Because I couldn't pronounce them'.

She smiled a little wintry smirk, 'logical and realistic, you have the position, when would you like to start?' She shook my hand. A phase of my life had ended and another was about to begin. My first day in RTE, 5 February 1964 was inauspicious. I sat opposite Síle's desk while she informed me of my duties, responsibilities and future. It seemed that my main task was to assist the Regional Officer in whatever way she would deem necessary. Just before lunch she said 'Now, Mr Dowling, what will we do with your name? All programme people here use the Irish form, what will you do?' The answer was inevitable. I would use the Irish form and so one day in the spring of 1964, Donncha O Dulaing was born and Denis Dowling was forever consigned to the quiet past. Marcus Hurley's dictum at Fords was right again! 'When the boss smells gas, we all smell gas.'

Until recently I've had an inordinate fear of visits to the doctor so you can imagine my fear when I was informed that even after interviews and a microphone test that I had one more hurdle to surmount before becoming a staff member of RTE. The letter of appointment bore the dreaded small print, 'subject to a medical test'.

I went reluctantly to the RTE medical man in St Patrick's Hill in Cork who suggested kindly that there was 'no need to be so nervous'. And then when all tests were over, he asked casually, 'Did you ever spend any time in hospital?' Fearful of losing my opportunity and very positively I replied, 'Never'. Without looking up he asked, 'did you take out your tonsils yourself?' My fleeting visit to hospital in Fermoy some 15 years earlier had caught up with me. 'I suppose it's so long ago you forgot,' he suggested. I nodded. Anyway, a brief spell in hospital was no deterrent. Not even a fib got in the way of progress. I had my job and it was pensionable!

I was taken on a tour of the premises where I met Joe Gibbons, the technical superintendent; Paddy O'Connor and Oliver O'Brien, two sound men, in every sense of the word; Douglas Gunne, the Balance and Control officer; Paddy Corcoran, the cleaner, who wooed pigeons on to the flat roof of the studios and who yodelled for pleasure; Ettie O'Mahony the secretarial assistant; Mrs Brady who made the tea; Paddy O'Keefe, the receptionist and, of course, Máire Ní Mhurchú my fellow programme assistant who would be joined sometime later by Uinsionn MacGruairc. The programme output at the time included *A Munster Journal, Annso's Ansúd sa Mhumhain, A Woman's World, Late But Light* and various children's programmes presented and compiled by Máire Ní Mhurchú. I began my career with a quite unintentional blunder. I really believed that broadcasters wore sheepskin coats, so I purchased a quite expensive one and hung it on the nearest hanger. I never knew that I was hanging from the Regional Officer's peg! It was much later that Ettie, the secretary, told me and put me in my own place!

My first broadcast was an unmemorable announcement for a programme called 'Conversations with Missionaries', one of Síle Ní Bhriain's occasional series with men and women who spent most of their working lives in Africa. Soon, however, I had *A Munster Journal*, a weekly digest of events and personalities and its counterpart in the Irish language *Anso's Ansúd Sa Mhumhain* thrust upon me and my new working life had really begun.

More than a year after my arrival in radio, I was fortunate to meet Eamon de Valera, President of Ireland, on a private visit to the home of my friend Mainchín Seoighe. Mainchín, who still lives in Tankardstown near Bruree in Co. Limerick, has been a friend of mine since boyhood days when he taught Irish to our Gaelic League classes in Charleville. He writes fluently in Irish and in English and is the great chronicler of his county. Since 1944 he has contributed a weekly article to the *Limerick Leader* using his pen-name 'An Mangaire Súgach', nickname for the famous Limerick poet, Aindrias MacCraith. Mainchín wrote a much-loved biography of Seán South *Maraíodh Seán Sabhat Aréir* as well as *Cois Máighe na gCaor* which dealt with the eighteenth-century poets of the Maigue.

Mainchín's mother, Nora, was a schoolmate of Eamon de Valera in Bruree and it was in her house I first met Dev. Without Mainchín there would have been no radio series on the schooldays of *A Boy from Bruree*. This fortuitous event led to far-reaching effects on my fledgling radio career. Many of my seniors in RTE became aware of me for the first time; some, those in posts senior to me in Dublin felt that I was too young, too inexperienced for the major series that followed, *Eamon de Valera, A Boy from Bruree*. Anyway, with the co-operation of Dev and the somewhat tardy blessing of my 'betters', I was launched on a very public career. The door to the private life of Ireland's senior statesman was unlocked and I was considered to be on the 'inside track' of Fianna Fáil. Not at all true! The series, apart from any intrinsic value, helped to confirm my own feelings about love of place and its significance in my own life.

I asked the President if his love for Bruree was important. His reply was a blueprint for much that followed for me in *Highways and Byways*.

> If you love your parish and your own little community you'll widen it so as to embrace the nation as a whole ... if you love your parish, you love your country.

* * *

During these early days I was delighted to meet 'Millie' whose 'My Boy Lollipop' was a huge success, as was sixteen-year-old Helen Shapiro, whose 'Walking Back To Happiness' led her to a long and successful singing career. When I met her she was as new as myself! The papers began to take notice, the late Maxwell Sweeney writing in the *Irish Independent* commented on a broadcast from the Festival of Kerry. 'It was odd to hear 'The Sash', one of the most popular of all orange ballads sung in a programme from Munster. Add to the oddity the fact that it was sung by a Dublin group, The Wolfe Tones and you have one of the entertaining contributions to the edition of *A Munster Journal* which covered the Festival of Kerry'. Maxwell went on to comment, 'some of the interviews might have been brighter'. How right he was.

One day recently, Brendan Balfe reminded me of another incident. Donncha has joined thousands of fans for a concert in the Savoy Cinema in Cork. Mick Jagger and the Rolling Stones are guests. Donncha wonders what he is doing backstage in the mid-sixties. Meanwhile in the tatty calm of the Radio Eireann Studios in Dublin, young Brendan Balfe is 'on continuity duties', one of those disembodied voices that appeared in between programmes and was prepared to play suitable music if anything broke down. Tonight was proving a little different. This was an outside broadcast and the Rolling Stones were giving a live interview to an unknown broadcaster. No breakdown occurred, except between the unlikely protagonists.

Brendan listened intently. This was scoop world. These fellows didn't give interviews. What was young O Dulaing up to? It was hardly vintage *Munster Journal*. He must have prepared himself? And then it started ....

'Mr Jagger, what brings you to Cork?'

'Concerts.'

You could feel the sweat and animosity.

'Tell me, Mr Jagger, would you be a pop band or a Rock n'Roll Band?'

'Blues, man, blues, we're a rhythm and blues band'

'Something like the Beatles then?'

'Naw, nothing like the Beatles, right?'

There were some musical interpolations like a honky-tonk version of Gounod's 'Ave Maria' with hints of unquiet desperation.

'Have you ever made records?', I asked.

Mick was beginning to fret a little!

'Yeah, yeah man a few. Do you know "Can't get no satisfaction"?'

Strange silence.

'Well no, actually, I used to collect Mario Lanza and Ronnie Ronald discs.'

Brendan thought, 'Now who is doing what to whom'. At this stage the interview was beginning to fall apart. Jagger was bristling.

'You don't seem to know very much about us, do you?'

'Well, no actually, should I ... by the way, where do you come from?'

'From London – ever hear of it?'

'Vaguely, I must thank you and your friends for a most informative and delightful chat here in Cork. I hope we meet again sometime.'

Sounds of applause emerged, both Mick and Donncha appeared to be laughing, retreating from what had been, for both, a deeply iconoclastic experience. If only I knew all that was to follow.

I was trained in the school of broadcasting which believed that the interviewer was merely a funnel through which information was passed on to the listener. It was certainly wrong for the presenter to force his own opinion or point of view on the subject, in other words, if you have a dog there is no need to bark for him! All of my early training in radio led this way and Paddy Downey much later on in his own column in *The Irish Times* referred to my contributions as being good but almost 'terse'. Old habits and traits live on.

A Munster Journal afforded me my first opportunities to travel the length and breadth of the province; it was my first attempt to give a definite voice to the hidden Ireland and has remained my objective ever since. I began to discover the world of the Irish Country Woman's Association and helped to provide new outlets for them in programmes like *Mid-Morning* and *A Woman's World* when I presented and produced it. Sterling women like Daphne Pochin Mould, Hilda Murphy, Maureen

Morrish, Christine Crowley and Mrs O'Flaherty, Liam's widow, and Leslie, Bean de Barra joined a regular team of broadcasters in the Cork Studios.

On Whit Monday 1964, I first met Richard Hayward, writer, balladeer, actor, orangeman and great Irishman on the summit of Galteemore in Co. Tipperary. It was a case of future events casting their shadows before them and my first exciting climb of real Irish mountain. Later that year, on Sunday 6 September, I had the pleasure of attending a medieval banquet in Bunratty Castle, Co. Clare to launch his monumental and interesting *Munster and the City of Cork*. On the strength of reading it, I recorded an edition of *A Munster Journal* in Gouganebarra where I met the Tailor's son for the first time and visited the oratory of St Finbarr and the little cemetery where the Tailor and Ansty lie together, as Hayward put it 'Peacefully at Last'.

The trauma and sadness of *The Tailor and Ansty*, by Eric Cross, closed forever like the misguided and misunderstood book he wrote about them. Seamus Murphy's granite stone says everything;

Tadhg O'Buachalla An Táilliúir 1860–1945

A Star Danced and Under that was I Born

Ainstí A Bhainchéile 1872–1947.

Tadhg O Buachalla, the tailor, and his wife Ainstí lived near Gouganebarra in West Cork. Eric Cross told the story of all the fun and laughter that rippled by their fireside in *The Tailor and Ansty*. Fame did not bring success to the innocent old couple. They were pilloried and vilified for their earthy attitudes to life and sexuality. Church and State condemned this innocent old couple and forced them to a life of isolation. Most of the neighbours abandoned the friendly hearth and only a few like Frank O'Connor remained to celebrate their lifestyle. The book was censored and even burned. To think of it today, brings a sour taste to the mouth and whenever I visit their grave I think of them. It is in many ways the 'other' side of that Ireland that I have celebrated all my life.

Síle Ní Bhriain guided me along the road to broadcasting. She opened to me every window to the world of Munster. Her own example, with her voice and broadcasting style, dark and silky in tone, could not but influence the tyro broadcaster. She advised, criticised and led. *Donal O Corcora Remembered* was my tribute to Daniel Corkery, the father of Munster and Irish writers. Not alone did he influence the likes of Seán O Faolain, Frank O'Connor and Seamus Murphy but his seminal work *The Hidden Ireland,* drove me far beyond the boundaries of town and city into the wilder, wider world that lay around. Before I was a year in the Cork studio Síle's prompting had guided me far from the world of Corkery and back towards the literary world of my university days, when I reflected on the first Teach-In held in UCC.

I think the epic stories of the 'Teach-In' are best left to the late Augustine Martin. Writing in the *Irish Press*, he was more than generous:

'The most exciting piece of Radio I have heard for many a day was in Donncha O Dulaing's finely edited report from the Cork "Teach-In" ... If you want to get the state of urgency, excitement and intensity of the occasion, tune in ....' He referred to recordings of Fr Brendan O'Mahony, OFM, Fr Fergal O'Connor OP, and Captain John Feehan of the Mercier Press. He remarked on Fr O'Connor's 'honesty' and frequently talked of 'this sense of prudent self-interest,' which Fr O'Connor concluded to be 'one of the greatest moral failings'. The critic concluded, 'Thank God it was given no sanctuary at the Cork Teach-in'. Others who took part in the broadcasts included Seán O Tuama, Edna O'Brien, Fr Peter Connolly, M J O'Kelly, Claude Cockburn. As Gus said we really exploded 'Dynamite from the South'.

I saw the role of radio expanding and with guests like Edna O'Brien and Fr Peter Connolly from Maynooth on *A Munster Journal*, the perimeters of radio possibilities extended to infinity. I decided that it was time to spread our wings to the Irish diaspora in England and so in December 1965 I headed for the Irish community in London. I hoped that while there I might visit the BBC in Broadcasting House. I did, spending some time with *Woman's Hour* under its editor Teresa McGonigle from Cobh and its famous presenter, Marjorie Anderson. It was a perfect example of a programme wedded to its audience but never constricted by its objectives. *Friday Night is Music Night*, a long-time favourite on the BBC Light Programme provided insights into the world of variety, radio and theatre audiences and the sheer style and skill of the medium at its best. The Camden Theatre provided the perfect locale for orchestras, brass bands, choirs, soloists and the inimitable presenter, Jimmy Kingsbury and led on inexorably to my own later series *On Stage In Cork*.

Around this time Norris Davidson, the head of the scriptwriters department in Dublin was casting around for a new member for his team. I was invited to join on a temporary basis and so my radio world reached back towards the birthplace of Irish broadcasting. Scriptwriters lived on the second floor of the General Post Office and were a unique and select enclave who carried their own keys into the building. You were left in no doubt that you might be joining the best. Norris presided. He had his own private office on the third floor. It was here that one learned of one's projects. My first day was somewhat unusual. Travelling up from Cork, I was at my desk at 9.30 a.m. No one else was! Aine McEvoy, who was secretary and mother-figure to Norris, Ciaran MacMathuna, Proinsias O Conluain, Seán MacReamoinn and PP Maguire was surprised but delighted to meet me.

'You're early', she said and put the kettle on. In due course the other scriptwriters gradually drifted in and I was hospitably brought to lunch in the Charcoal Grill just down O'Connell Street and above the Carlton Cinema. Miss Griffin presided and my new colleagues had a special table. It was very far away from RTE in Union Quay. The telephone rang, Aine said, 'It's Norris. I'll bring you up to him'. I was thrilled to meet the great man and well aware of his reputation as a documentary maker on both film and radio, having read of his association with the great Grierson and some of the finest broadcasts of their type. Norris sat me down in the tiny office and I found myself staring at a lurid circus poster. 'When could you start work?' he asked. As usual I said, 'now'.

He looked at me quizzically and said, 'I would like you to write, present and compile a short series which we will call, *A Corkman's Dublin*. These will be half an hour's duration each and will begin in three weeks'. From my experience in Cork, this seemed a long time. 'I would suggest some reading', he said, perhaps Seán O'Casey's autobiographies, a flick through Joyce and so on'. He advised me to develop my own style and to write to be read out loud and heard, presenting me with a copy of his pamphlet, *This Business of Scriptwriting*. He mentioned casually that Frank, Francis McManus who had been Head of Features or Features Officer as he was known, had considered my documentary on Daniel Corkery to be 'workmanlike and enjoyable'. I glowed. Compliments did not flow freely in Scriptwriters. He sent me away with the instruction to 'let me see the script before you record' – a dash of cold realism! To make a long story short, I walked Dublin, morning, noon and evening, soaking in the glowing atmosphere of summer days, imbibing past resonances of dusty streets, blank stones and green parks.

I felt it along the blood, I read its writers, joined in its songs and wrote of it all through the eyes of a young Corkman. Norris read my script, smiled and said cryptically, 'very Augustan, homework done, scriptwriters' material' ... I was accepted. The critics were more wary, 'stilted and somewhat mannered', said one, another found it 'rewarding listening', while yet another considered that I had found a city 'full of toffee apples and Joe Lynch'. As for me, I fell under the spell of Dublin and would never be quite the same again. My window which looked out over Henry Street and towards Cole's Lane with its echoes of Sean O'Casey and the dying O'Rahilly focused on the ever-shifting, ever-changing panorama of Moore Street. I can still see on those summer days in the mid-sixties a Chekhovian old man who stood all day holding a sad bunch of artificial flowers.

My learning curve was soaring and, within months I had three other major broadcasting opportunities. I combined with Norris Davidson in a radio feature dealing with the famous Mitchelstown Caves. Much of this was recorded underground in the days before lighting was acquired for the dark depths of this weird underworld. Tommy O'Brien, then radio critic with the Cork *Evening Echo,* was intrigued with the broadcasting combination and wrote of 'Norris Davidson and Donncha O'Dulaing – a widely contrasting pair'. This had been my third opportunity to combine with senior scriptwriters.

Earlier in my young career I had worked with PP Maguire in two broadcasts recorded in the Co. Galway area; one, *Yeats in Ballylee* and the second which told of the founding of the Abbey Theatre, was called *The Count at Duras* which reminds me of several futile attempts to wed city and country culture. The locals around Kinvara found PP Maguire's style of questioning difficult to comprehend. PP was a little lost and I provided some interpretative balance.

PP: 'Would you say that the Count of Duras was a very gregarious man?'

Local person: 'What's he saying?'

But, for all that, Maguire's skills as programme maker and my own growing expertise as interviewer made for a lively combination and PP soon joined us in Cork as Acting Head during one of Síle Ní Bhriain's bouts of illness. Once again I was fortunate in those who worked around me and the learning process continued. The time had come, however, to make up my mind and, without too much soul-searching I decided to return to Cork. When I came back I found Síle Ní Bhriain much changed. Her own broadcasting lights were fading, but she continued to offer opportunities to her team, even though an undeclared policy of secessional attitudes to Henry Street was obvious. The variety of programming emanating from the Cork studios was quite extraordinary although much of the credit for this must go to the controller of programmes in Dublin, Riobaird O Farachán, the poet and scholar who held the reins of radio during exceedingly difficult times when television arrived and radio stood beleaguered, losing its public and its best to the new medium. There was most definitely a clearly etched line of antipathy and dislike between the two services. 'Radio Eireann' and 'Telefís Eireann' were poles apart. Síle often referred to television as 'the junior service', a service which prospered from an ongoing haemorrhaging of the best talent in Henry Street into the bloodstream of Montrose.

There were, however, certain consolations. Without the departures of Gerry Murray and others from the Cork Studios, my arrival and continuing prosperity in radio might never have happened. A two-way mirror of opportunity existed for talent. Síle's health problems increased. She was now in St Vincent's Hospital in Dublin and when I called to see her I was shocked. I hardly recognised her. Only her spirit remained undimmed. Her skeletal appearance belied her planning session as she sat with me and discussed next year's plans, a year that she would never see. She shook my hand firmly but we never said goodbye. She reminded me of some forms that needed completion in Cork, enquired of my family's welfare and shortly afterwards I left. Her influence on me and the sound of her great broadcasting voice remain vivid to the present day. Difficult and set in her ways she may have been, but a more honest and supportive friend I shall never meet. Such people are the heartbeat of radio.

Síle's death and my appointment as Regional Officer in the Cork studio in Union Quay heralded new times and new departures. It was time to open new doors, time to reach out to a public up to now held at one remove. Radio would no longer be what two little girls had once described it to me – 'all Irish and fiddles'. Uinsionn MacGruairc, by now a skilful and competent broadcaster, adopted and adapted to himself the role of the 'Irish language' expert among us. His Kerry blas, exquisite and mellifluous, was heard to great advantage in many series. A sharp but not unkind intelligence allied to a rapier-sharp sense of humour made him an ideal communicator in changing times. Máire Ní Mhurchú continued to wheedle and encourage numerous series for the schoolchildren of Munster and has, in fact, never been replaced in that role. As for me, well with confidence unbounded I set out to spread the radio gospel far and wide. I made myself available for talks on broadcasting to groupings here, there and everywhere.

I travelled one evening to Doneraile to remind them of earlier broadcasts dealing with 'Canon Sheehan of Doneraile' and a feature dealing with the St Leger family. Each gathering concluded with a recording for *Mid Morning* which radio slot I shared with the scriptwriters of Dublin. I recognised in the ICA a great grassroots and practical force for good and allied myself to them. Jean Sheridan, writing in the *Irish Press* attended one of these gatherings. To my surprise she found that 'if Richard Dimbleby is the voice of Imperial Britain then Donncha O Dulaing of

Radio Eireann is the voice of genuine Munster'. Inaccurately but prophetically she wrote, 'He does not want to be anything else'. Her description is close, not too close! 'Cheerful, round-faced and bespectacled, he suggests both student and schoolmaster'. It was at this time that I met Maeve Curtis for the first time. She was then a journalist with the *Cork Examiner* and suggested that I might join her on a visit to Termonfeckin, Co Louth, the summer college of the ICA. This was far outside my Cork brief, but I was the boss and rules were easily broken. So, I carried my gospel of radio for the people to a communications course in the college. Within a couple of years, I would conduct such courses myself. Maeve was delighted and I was soon an integral part in the life of a great national organisation. I once remember travelling to Sligo to a huge ICA meeting where I recorded *Mid Morning*. I brought with me my regular team of Christine Crowley, Hilda Murphy and Maureen Morrish who were as wired to the system as myself and absolutely brilliant talkers and great communicators.

By now the time had come to invite the public into the radio centre and I devised a new radio series *On Stage In Cork*. These programmes took place before full houses in the Cork School of Music Concert Hall and were presented and produced by myself and loosely based on *Friday Night is Music Night*. The audiences overflowed on to the stage and tickets were always at a premium. RTE Cork had certainly gone public. My guests included Liam Devally, Brendan O Cíobháin, John Carolan, Donal Ring's Ceili Band, John McConville, Deirdre O'Callaghan, St Finbarr's Male Voice Choir, the beginnings of Cha and Miah, talkers, dancers and the great Concert Hall Chorale. We recorded on Saturday nights during *The Late Late Show* time and these I really enjoyed! The best of all worlds lay before me. I was lecturing in the country, controlling a unique and virile radio studio and broadcasting. My cup was full, but time, Cork time was running out.

Brave New Flawed World

The wind seemed at my back when Oliver Maloney, then Director of Personnel, invited me to join a Radio Steering Committee with the special objective of changing the face of radio, leading to longer hours and greater flexibility. Tom Hardiman, who was Director General was absolutely in favour of change and improvement. Indeed, being a former 'Henry Street man', he had never forgotten his radio roots.

The Committee consisted of Kevin Roche, PP Maguire and myself with Oliver as Chairman and Michael Carroll as Secretary. We spent a long time consulting, agonising and debating and ultimately came up with a schedule which was acceptable to Riobaird O Farachain, Controller of Programmes and his assistant Michael O hAodha.

Programmes I remember planning include *Sunday Miscellany* and *Music For Middlebrows*, both still healthy, lively and running. There was much heart-searching and much blood-letting and not a little hurt as many people lost their places and were devastated while others gained position and were glad. There is no easy road to change.

At the end of it all I suddenly found myself appointed Head Of Features and Current Affairs while still retaining the Regional Officer's post in Cork. My department encompassed features, current affairs, religion and agriculture, obviously a major and heavy burden which I accepted with excitement and delight. I was also much younger than any other departmental head and carried little baggage from my very brief time in Henry Street as a member of scriptwriters.

There was little welcome for me among the senior members of my staff, some of whom either felt they ought to have got the job or considered me an upstart from Cork, politically well-aligned and no fit person to succeed Francis McManus. The atmosphere in the long corridor was a little strained. To paraphrase *Gone With The Wind*, I didn't give a damn!

Many of the newspaper critics took their cue from Henry Street sources and also doubted my ability. Enemies once made are made forever, enmity once engendered never diminishes.

Proinsias O Conluain, once a scriptwriter, was one of the few who formally welcomed me. I have never forgotten him for it. I remember early meetings with my staff where new enthusiasms began to grow, except for the odd member who slept soundly! I began to cast about for newcomers and discovered Freda McGough whose fine voice and broadcasting talent extend to this present day.

Annette Andrews, then an announcer, played a major role in the new schedule while Terry Prone and the late Christina Murphy shone in programmes for young people.

Over the years I had been an admirer of BBC Radio's *Sports Report* and among their presenters was Liam Nolan from Cobh. One day I met him in London and he expressed a desire to return home. I took him at his word and he took me at mine and returned to present *Here and Now* and *The Liam Nolan Hour* for starters. His style and image helped to change the face of daytime radio and I am proud that I brought him home. He was the big success of my part in the schedule. Lest I forget, I should mention three of my all-time favourite broadcasters, Andy O'Mahony and John Bowman whose diligence and skill have them in the first rank in their field; and of course the ubiquitous Brendan Balfe whose broadcasting talent and creative skills were quite prodigious even then.

Editorial Board Meetings became central to my management life. Riobaird O Farachain presided over schedule planning, policy and forward planning and assessment of the service. Tom Hardiman made several appearances and played an active and vigilant part in radio. It was here, too, that I first met Michael O'Hehir, then Head of Sport. I was still a fan and I remember saying to the Controller that Michael's presence was like having all my boyhood dreams come true.

To this day I have never ceased being a radio fan and the magic of broadcasting is always with me. As part of development we felt that radio might gain from a closer association with television and so we planned a bold and original stroke, the continuation of *The Late Late Show* by extending its topics into a *Later than Late* radio show in Henry Street. The idea was for Gay Byrne to hand over to Bunny Carr, who was to present the new radio show, at the conclusion of *The Late Late Show* with a hoped-for boost in radio listening from the backwash of television. There was a meeting held in the Montrose Hotel to discuss arrangements. It was attended by Maeve Conway-Piskorski, then my counterpart on television, Gay Byrne, Bunny Carr and myself. For one reason or another the idea never fired and the hoped-for handover remained a dream.

I have been Gay's guest on the *Late Late* at least three times in my career, the first around that time. I had the thankless job of promoting and defending RTE Radio's Irish language policy. It was a daunting task to look at an audience, many of whose positions in radio I had changed and all of whom had the word 'anti' written across their faces. Fortunately for RTE and indeed, myself my ideas were quite similar to those of my protagonists and by the end of the discussion they were left in no doubt as to my good intentions. One of their number, Aidin Ni Chaoimh swiftly became presenter of a new current affairs programme. I was even able to talk of the Director General's and my own plans to devise bilingual meetings within the halls of Henry Street and to a lesser extent in Donnybrook. This was not too difficult on radio as tradition and training, not to say requirement for entry to the organisation, were Irish in the orientation and style. Radio bred an Irishness in act and thought that was unique. Tom Hardiman believed, as I did, that our national language should come from the heart. Furthermore, it seemed fairly logical to assume that those who trumpeted on and on about 'the first language of the state' would be proficient in that same language and comfortable in their role within an organisation where the Irish language lived and was not fettered by out-moded ideas or practices. We believed that Irish should be spoken rather than spoken about in Henry Street. We eschewed the academic approach and avoided 'cultural' programmes where the national language became a crutch for semi-retired academics. The Director General hoped that at least half the business of the editorial board would be conducted through Irish. It was a very brave aspiration which, unfortunately never came to fruition. Still, we tried.

The vivid commemoration of the 1916 Rebellion in 1966 was celebrated without fear of failure. Memories of the Rising and graphic descriptions of the happenings, well-laced with national songs were the order of the day. It seemed that we could not get enough of this material and I must say that RTE reflected well my own thinking and ambitions. 'Ireland not only free but Gaelic' never needed to be said!

Then came the Northern civil rights movement and all changed. Now we were not merely reflecting the wars and dreams of the past, but holding our broadcasting mirror up to bloody and uncompromising reality. For some, high-minded attitudes prevailed and words like 'freedom', 'democracy' and 'objectivity' were thrown about and often misused. Our critical faculties were disarmed by our own lack of serious intent to truly reflect the horrendous and brutal happenings now so close to us.

What a BBC Director General in another context described as a 'malignant, inefficient, dwarfish bureaucracy, intent on censorship', swiftly grew up. Songs, beloved by our own ancestors, were dropped without a trace. Thomas Davis, creator of so much verse, had his own words often attenuated and the much maligned 'Government Censorship' became 'self-censorship'. Giving the public what it wanted and 'democracy' and 'trusting the people' became a fearful and cowardly form of broadcasting where many led from the back and broadcasters floundered between the sentimental patriotism of the early and mid-sixties and the need to seriously reflect present events. 'What the people needed' and what we gave often created a fiction of lower standards and less than truth in presentation.

There were, however, notable and noteworthy exceptions. On two succeeding Sundays my Features and Current Affairs Department presented two hour-long programmes, *Derry 69* and *Belfast 69*. A broadcasting team set off for each city and by transmission time on Sunday morning, having worked through Friday and Saturday nights we were ready. My trip to Derry city in August 1969 came at the height of the new 'troubles' in that city. The episode signalled a muscle-flexing exercise from the Features and Current Affairs department when I felt that it was time to reflect the fast-moving happenings in that troubled city. My team was chosen with care: Nollaig McCarthy, Howard Kinlay, Michael Littleton, Seán MacRéamoinn and myself. It was a new departure for a Departmental Head to lead from the front but that was how it would be.

Nollaig McCarthy drove our hired car and after two exchanges with B Specials who were armed with Sten guns and knew where to point them, we reached our target. Derry, the Bogside and Creggan in particular were under siege. Over the city hung a cloud of gas while the atmosphere was tense with fear and foreboding. The civilian population on the Catholic side had spent days and nights repelling RUC and B Specials. Terror and anger were written on every face while the British army, recently drafted in by the Government, was given a warm if nervous welcome by the civilian population. It was, to put it mildly, bizarre.

We decided to split our team and then to meet and discuss the tactics. Our main objective was to return with local impressions of what appeared to be a very confused situation. Michael Littleton approached Eddie McAteer, great seminal voice of the Nationalist movement in the six counties, who set the scene:

> This all began on 29 March 1613 when the Honorable Irish Society got possession of the ancient city of Derry and when they gave us this humiliating prefix London ... Derry. The siege mentality had existed since then. Colonials have been against the natives and this lasted right down through that long time.

McAteer looked across the troubled cityscape where places like Butcher's Gate and Ship Quay Gate, reflected their troubled history.

> Derry is the Danzig of the North. Things are so blatantly wrong here that
> it provides a rallying cry for the rest of the six counties. We have a two to
> one majority, yet have been continually helpless in our own city.

He reflected on traditional Unionist thinking from the controversial walls of Derry. 'They are above and we are below, the haves and have-nots, the non-assimilating colonials and natives.'

Eamon McCann, the young socialist activist, talked freely to the late Howard Kinlay, 'The real enemy here is the system that the RUC and the B Specials represent.' Unemployment for men ran at some 40 per cent in Catholic areas. The working class, to use his own expression were frustrated, demoralised and without hope. Howard hopefully suggested a role for 'the South'. The reply was trenchant and astounding at that time to my ears.

> Our problems will not be solved simply by joining the South, what we
> need is a big change internally in the south to parallel the changes we are
> calling for in the North – the destruction of Toryism both North and South.

My 'romantic Ireland' perceptions were taking a roasting. When it came to looking for leadership from any of the churches, McCann was equally trenchant.

> The Catholic and Protestant Bishops have called for calm, but they, like
> many others, are out of touch with the people. I was quite pleased to see
> Dr Farren (the Catholic Bishop) walk through the Bogside. I was 26 years
> of age and it was the first time that I had ever seen a Bishop walking
> through any Catholic area of the town.

Seán Mac Réamoinn's approach was somewhat more academic as was his Church of Ireland interviewee, Canon McKechnie. Seán suggested that more Protestants than Catholics were employed in Derry because there were more Protestant employers. He received a nod. The canon concluded:

> It is rather unfortunate that we are in the upper part of the town, literally
> looking down on the Bogside. It may have a psychological effect on those
> who live there, a very undesirable thing. I don't like ghettos.

Seán turned his attention to the Catholic side of the divide. Fr AJ Coulter was equally certain in his ideas. 'I must point out that the Catholic schools do not go out of their way, or indeed specifically inculcate a nationalist, still less a republican philosophy among their pupils.' What a place of certainties! 'The two sides do not fully trust each other ... yet.' Change takes a little time!

Nollaig McCarthy and I walked through the Creggan. We met a young husband and wife standing red-eyed and fearful at their doorway. They told a sorry tale of the RUC on the rampage, 'Rattling their shields and shooting tear-gas indiscriminately into little houses when innocent families tried to sleep.'

I wondered if they had any hopes. 'Oh yes,' the woman said, 'we heard your leader, Mr Lynch say that they will help us from the south and it is said that the Free State Army is already at the Border. What a welcome they'll get in the Creggan.' Everywhere confusion and misinformation reigned. Even Ivan Cooper seemed distraught in his approach. This is not a revolution,' he said:

> it is more of a preservation. Paisleyites, B Specials and police are the enemies here. If this is sectarian, then the Unionist party have made it that way. Real civil war could happen tomorrow.

Like most people we met, he was beside himself with frustration.

Michael Littleton questioned Eddie McAteer about the reception for the British Army. 'It's a relative welcome,' he said. 'There is a terrible hatred here of the police force and, of course of the B Specials. Any kind of devil is more welcome than the RUC.'

Later on I met with Fr Edward Daly, later to be bishop of Derry. He spoke with certitude and conviction. I asked him about ongoing injustice. 'There has always been injustice in Derry,' he said.

> Right from the foundation of the police, it's been like this ... young people who have never worked in their lives with no prospect of ever working and all the hopelessness and frustration that goes with it.

He was sad and exhausted but willing to talk. 'The Bogside is the North of Ireland in miniature, all of its dreadful reality.' We talked of civil rights. His sadness and truth touched me as never before.

> For 40 years or more people have complained about injustice. They have engaged in peaceful protest, trying to make people outside the North aware of what is going on, appealing to Stormont even with every kind of appeal except in a violent way.

I wondered if fear and hopeless resentment could be contained any longer where law and order have completely broken down. Fr Daly spoke slowly and with emphasis:

> As a priest, it's very difficult to say this, but one must say it, the people have no confidence in the RUC. In my mind and with what I have seen here, their hatred and fears are justified.

I wondered again about the tea and biscuits given with kind words to the British army. Fr Daly said:

> The British soldiers were welcomed as an alternative to the RUC, but I think that Derry people look forward at some time to a United Ireland and while British faces are accepted now, they certainly do not form a solution

to the problems of Derry, they are merely a temporary solution .... Eddie
McAteer said it yesterday when he said that people would have welcomed
the Devil himself as a viable alternative.

We talked quietly then of Jack Lynch, An Taoiseach's address on the 9.00
television news on RTE and his promise that we in the South would not
stand by. Fr Daly was unambiguous, 'it electrified the place. I was there
around 9.15 when the news began spreading'. I asked, tentatively about
attitudes towards help from the Republic. He smiled, 'They have felt very
much isolated, because for many years we had come to believe that people
in Dublin had forgotten about us.'

On that note of optimism in August 1969, our radio team headed back
for Dublin. It was a balmy Saturday night and a civil rights meeting was
taking place at the GPO. Micheál O hAodha was waiting to welcome us
home. We were an event! After tea and sandwiches sent from the
Gresham, we worked through the night and the following Sunday
morning 18 August 1969, *Derry 1969* was broadcast.

To make a very long story short, with the wreaking of internment on
the North and what I believed to be our less than honest concerns in the
Republic, I became very nervous and disillusioned. With the approach of
Christmas 1971, the first Christmas of internment, I decided to do
something about it. I set out to organise 5,000 toys for internees' children
for Christmas and through newspapers, broadcasts on radio and
nationwide contacts decided to go for it.

My radio colleagues in Henry Street, including Mick McKeever and
Tommy Ryan were most generous and helpful and Joe Jennings of CIE
became an indispensable part of our efforts. Through him CIE opened up
to us a large store at the Five Lamps in Dublin and the great toy journeys
of 1971 began. I contacted the Central Citizens Defence Committee in
Belfast and the late Mr Tom Conaty and they were charmed with the idea
and a date was set. I saw the toy train off but did not travel.

Pressures were somewhat intense as my use of the national
broadcasting service as a collecting agency was less than welcome, so I
decided, partly because I felt unwell and partly from fear of retribution in
RTE, to stay at home. A great and cheerful crowd set out that morning and
I knew that success was assured. One of the papers headlined 'Toy Train
Special From The South' and chronicled our efforts, telling the story of a
child from Thurles named Meagher who went to a toyshop and said, 'here
are all my Christmas presents, give them to the children of internees in
Belfast'. This was symbolic of the whole country. I was thrilled that we
had stimulated a great national outpouring of generosity and decided to go
quietly to Belfast on the Christmas Eve. I spent a great day with mothers

and children and saw a little of their lives first hand. We helped to brighten a little of the Christmas of 1971.

Imagine my surprise when I returned from Belfast to find a telegram waiting from the Controller of Programmes, telling me to visit the home of an RTE Senior Executive. I did. He was most welcoming but left me in no doubt as to RTE's attitude to the 'Santa Claus Train'. Everyone knew that I was generous but everyone also knew that the 'toys' were not an advisable move for the Head of Features and Current Affairs, never mind using his own medium as publicity for the project. I was silent and shocked but worse was to follow. It was further suggested that my Belfast contacts were 'probably fronts for the Provisional IRA'. I knew they were not fronts for anyone except fatherless children. I was saddened and furious. I had no knowledge of anyone, connected personally or otherwise, with the Provisional IRA. My destruction by isolation, whether by accident or design, had begun.

He offered me a glass of whiskey and we drank to 'a happy Christmas.' Christ help us! I spent that holiday planning my imminent resignation as Head of Features and drafting a letter to the national newspapers.

A terrible isolation had begun. A few of those who had worked for me and with me quickly stepped back. With one or two notable exceptions, others who had shared my thoughts and dreams avoided me. I was bitterly alone. My national sympathies and ideas were suspect. I was disliked, probably feared. Survival was more honoured than progress. The 'national' question and those with the tag 'nationalist' or, horror of horrors, 'republican' were to be removed. 'Safety' was cherished while the pale spectre of self-censorship and cowardice moved through the service.

The other day I came across my old copy of *The Country Girls* and I found within it a letter written to me by Edna O'Brien. She was as distraught as myself. It all reminds me of her journey with me to Derry and of her kindness and generosity to my friends in that city. She remained there for some days and this short excerpt from her letter bears witness to desolation. She writes of:

> a most eventful trip. It is a sad sad and nearly insoluble situation ... I hardly know what to do next ....

Thank you Edna, you were one of the few who really did and whose kindness was real and meaningful.

Still, time passed and I put much of my anger and sadness behind me until just before another Christmas when my star seemed to be on the ascendant and a major television programme beckoned.

Years, later a young and very talented producer seemed to signal some sort of rehabilitation. 'You know,' he said. 'I think they were all wrong about you. We were told that you were very difficult to work with. That's not true. You were always labelled as a heavy drinker and an IRA man.' There was a startled pause. Truth rarely emerges with such starkness. He was surprised at his own temerity. I was shocked but not surprised. He was merely expressing the demonisation which had taken place. It was comforting to actually hear it clearly expressed. The twin faces of prejudice and cowardice were certainly bared. It was as I always thought. I was like the great national songs, never banned, but quietly laid aside.

I told Oliver Maloney of my ideas concerning resignation. He was kind, understanding and helpful. He advised caution and asked me if I knew what I was doing. Here I was, father of a young family, resigning from one of the best jobs in the land. I knew all this and I knew the inherent dangers of stepping away from power. However, I joined Radio Eireann to become a broadcaster and not a manager, so I put it down on paper! That was it. I was a man outside the pale, but as always in broadcasting, the world turns around and, before very long, times would change and I would quite forget much of the trauma of 1971 and move on.

Before closing the pages on 1971, it's worth remembering that I played a major part in setting up Radio na Gaeltachta. Once more under the guidance of Tom Hardiman, men and women of goodwill strove to widen the perimeters of our national language. The people of RTE who set the wheels in motion should never be forgotten. Ni fheicfear a leithéid arís'. I applied for the post of 'Ceannaire' in the new organisation. I got a formal note informing me of my rejection. The Director General had added a footnote in his own handwriting.

> Ná bíodh buairt ort faoin toradh seo. Sar-chnaoltóir thú: tá an-chuid le déanamh agat in RTÉ.

How kind of him to bring hope when the 'slough of despond' was closing around me, ach bhí laetheanta eile le teacht agus gan mhoill.

Incidentally, a massive anti-O Dúlaing campaign had been mounted by various elements within and without Radio na Gaeltachta. The fact that I might have been among their few friends in the Henry Street establishment went unacknowledged. It was certainly a flawed world now, but I was not done, not by a long chalk!

For a time I retreated within myself. I even indulged in that most useless of emotions, regret. My thoughts and my actions were fractious. I allowed time and prospects to slip by, not, mind you, without the assistance of some of my former friends.

I remember one day standing in Donnybrook when my despair and isolation were at their peak. Pádraic O Rathallaigh and his wife, Peig Monahan, were driving by and saw me. He stopped his car and came over to me on the kerbside. He spoke words of encouragement, which he probably does not now remember and there and then helped me to turn a corner in my life.

Highways and Byways

Three-O-One began as a back-handed gesture to me for my resignation as Head of Features and Current Affairs. I believed that as former head of the department and as presenter/producer since the beginnings of my broadcasting days in Cork, that I would present and produce the new series. This was not the case.

The loss of my 'headship' did not bother me until Micheál O'hAodha imparted unexpected and, to me, unwelcome news. 'John Skehan will be your editor', he said. I never spoke. The following morning John arrived. We were to share the great desk that up to then I had taken for myself. He was brusque and nervous as he informed me that programme and policy would be dictated by him. I think that he was as uncomfortable as I was, but we got on with it. I had already chosen the name *Three-O-One*. He informed me curtly that he had asked Brendan Balfe to choose the signature tune and, Brendan, with his usual enthusiasm and skill made a magnificent choice, 'Flower Among Them All', a Scottish tune played by Horslips.

This had been John's first decision and it set the tone for all that was to follow. A trust that slowly began between us, fairly soon developed into a warm and creative relationship. We quickly decided on a format for *Three-O-One* and the very first programme, an amalgam of the arts, folklore and literature set the scene for what almost invariably followed.

I travelled to London and persuaded Edna O'Brien to read from *The Country Girls* which we serialised. There was much soul-searching about it as many felt that we were breaking the law as the book was then on the banned list. Still, I argued that this was for the spoken rather than the written word and all passed off without a problem.

Looking now at the RTE Archive, I am stunned by the variety and scope of our material. Andy Allen, the memory man from Aughrim in Co. Wicklow sits easily with Kingsley Amis, the novelist. I was delighted, too, to talk with Arthur Askey who had been one of my heroes on *Radio Fun* and in the *Light Programme*. General Tom Barry and his wife Leslie, then in the Irish Red Cross, talked of how and where they met and were unplanned precursors to *The Boys of Kilmichael*, a radio documentary broadcast in 1970, fifty years after the event.

Elmer Bernstein, the American composer talked to us of 'The Magnificent Seven' and many other achievements. Kathleen Behan celebrated her ninetieth birthday in 1979 and my microphone was there in the Embankment to record the event which was Behanesque in every way. As the programme was being announced, Kathleen launched into 'The Tri-Coloured Ribbon' by her brother Peadar Kearney and no one seemed to listen to anyone else. Ulick O'Connor spoke with great affection and I, like him, remember visits to her in hospital. Rory Furlong, her son, left us in no doubt as to what constituted a rebel song.

Around this time too, I attended a Bogside Festival in Derry where I recorded set dancing as rubber bullets flew up and stones flew down. The programme was never transmitted. It was considered 'not suitable'. John was uncomfortable but doing his job. I asked myself my usual question 'was it for this wild geese spread the grey wing?'

We travelled to Denmark and Finland and had great radio adventures. The travel section, parsimonious as usual booked us into a cheap, clean hotel where the rooms, more like cubicles in fact, had wafer-thin walls. I never slept a wink. It seemed a very busy place with comings and goings all night. The following day we had lunch at the Irish embassy and, on hearing where we were staying, the ambassador's staff effected a quick change! It was my only stay in a brothel!

Finland was more exciting. We attended a great concert in the Sibelius Hall in Helsinki and travelled up to the Arctic Circle at Rovaniemi. Someone in Dublin told John Skehan that the Finns always carried spare footwear with them when visiting or entering houses. We took our cue from this and always arrived through the snow carrying our shoes in plastic bags. Our hosts had never heard of this idea! I interviewed one man who had taken part in the 'Hundred Days War' against the Soviets. Listening to him I might have been at home in west Cork talking to one of Barry's Flying Column.

Around this time, too, I visited London and met for the first time Patrick Galvin, the Cork poet. His stories of his travels and his reading of his verse remain sharply etched in my mind. I remember, in particular, his strange Cork/London accent as he half-read, half-declaimed 'The Mad Woman Of Cork'. The last verse is of immense power and suggestion:

> I am the madwoman of Cork
> Go away from me.
> And if I die now
> Don't touch me.
> I want to sail in a long boat
> From here to Roche's Point

And there I will anoint the sea
With oil of alabaster
I am the madwoman of Cork
And today is the feast day of Saint Anne
Feed me.

– poetry truly written for reading out loud and the very stuff of radio. Patrick has featured many and many a time in my broadcasts since then.

John B Keane from Listowel was visited and regaled me with his tales of Jones, the Chemist in Doneraile. Jones had made his name with a singular mixture called simply 'Jones, Scour Specific' and John B spent much of his time in Doneraile blending this unique cure which brought health to many an animal for years afterwards.

Leo Maguire was among my best loved guests and his voice was easily identified and carried with it warm echoes of Radio Eireann's sponsored programme days. I can still hear, 'If you feel like singing do sing an Irish song' as he brought the Walton-sponsored programme to an inevitable and tuneful conclusion. His own songs, like 'The Whistling Gypsy' are as unforgettable as himself.

Seamus Murphy, the sculptor from Cork, brought his talent, living and vivid into the studio with mystical elements of his own philosophy and art. Once, outside the radio studio and in his own studio in Cork, we looked at his work. He touched his bust of General Tom Barry and smiled, 'he was very patient ... a most interesting man. I don't have to tell you that'. He didn't! He looked around him at Dev, The Tailor, Sean O'Riada, Máirtín O Cadhain, John Montague, Maurice Walsh and the Countess. I wondered what would happen if all his sculptures spoke! 'What a way to be remembered', he said, almost without thinking, 'Twas Daniel Corkery influenced me most'. I think now – what a way to be remembered!

Three-O-One passed away. RTE planners in their ineffable wisdom changed the programme time to quarter past three. John Skehan stepped back and I thank him for all the fun, the creativity, the blending of outside broadcast with studio and above all else, his honesty. I often think of him. May he rest in peace, and if voices are heard in heaven, his is best.

* * *

Highways and Byways, my own choice of title, was born and grew to become a broadcasting legend in and beyond its own time. There was hardly a village or a road in Ireland which did not touch us. It was our intention to visit and record the lives of real people the length and breadth of Ireland. Like Seamus Murphy, Corkery's *Hidden Ireland* had a huge impact on me and the philosophy was carried through to *Highways and Byways*.

I suppose few of us can forget the Papal visit in 1979. I travelled to Rome before the visit in a state of great excitement to a Papal Audience in St Peter's Square when I stood near a vast crowd from Limerick who sang 'There is an Isle'. I held my microphone near Pope John Paul II as he looked at their banner which said 'Limerick'. Like the good pro that he is, he paused and said, 'next week I will be with you in Limerick'. The blood was up and Conor O'Clery of *The Irish Times* said 'you have a scoop'. The late Larry Lyons, an old friend from the *Cork Examiner* had a 'contact' or so he thought. We never did get into the Vatican apartments. But well tried Larry!

We did, however, visit San Clemente, the Roman home of the Irish Dominicans where the hospitality flowed as sweetly as in their Irish House in St Mary's in Tallaght. There was an old priest sitting on my right and we talked. 'What's your name?' I asked. 'Heuston', he said. 'As in station?' I jokingly asked. He looked at me quietly. 'Yes', he replied, 'his brother'. I topped up with multitudinous cups of black coffee and before the night was over one of the great occasions on *Highways and Byways* had taken place.

The papal flight to Dublin was unique. Tape machine in hand, I braved the international pack of paparazzi and legitimate Irish journalists and photographers who surged towards the Pope. I taped a few unmemorable words and was photographed by Pat Langan of *The Irish Times* and with him I thank Hubert Gordon of the Gardaí, who brilliantly secured everyone! Flying in low over the Phoenix Park over a Dublin still and empty apart from the huge throng in the park was a moving experience.

Liam Nolan and I were soon to describe another huge event as North came South to greet the Pope in Drogheda. By now I was not just hungover but exhausted and finding it hard to force out descriptive words. Liam, who was armed with a missal and much research material was in full flow. I was not at the races! Until, suddenly, it struck me. I had shared something with the Holy Father that morning that no one else had. I turned to Liam and said, 'do you know, Liam, that I shared black puddings for breakfast with the Pope this morning?' I was up and running and the rest of my commentary was sweet.

Cathal O Griofa, who was the editor of *Highways and Byways* set off with me across the 'the quiet land of Eireann' through the long night on to our sacred destination, the holy place at Clonmacnoise, the ancient home of St Ciaran. The Pope was about to pay a private visit here and I would be the only commentator privileged to broadcast from this place.

The dawn was grey and cold which made the tea all the more welcome as was the splendid poitín shared with me by a kindly, uniformed pilgrim. The quiet of the early morning was gently disturbed by thousands of feet walking the tiny roads of Clonmacnoise. Among them my own family, whom I met later in the field. The walking, driving, cycling throng loomed up out of the grey mist of dawn, surprising the quiet and sleepy Offaly cows that woke ruminating to a morning of history and a morning repeating itself because many generations had trodden these roads in times past. William Bulfin in his *Rambles in Eireann* re-draws the scene in words as only he can:

> On all the roads between Banagher and Athlone there are troops of people facing Westward. They are vehicles of every kind, from the dashing excursion break to the humble donkey cart, and every kind of bicycle procurable is also in evidence. Hundreds of people are tramping the roads in the dust; hundreds are footing it over the fields and the hills; and there are many boats on the Shannon all laden to the very gunwales with people from Connaght.

So William Bulfin described a 'Pattern' in his own time. It was great to be part of that great throng of history and now writing and saying our own chapters in the ongoing story of Clonmacnoise. It was a morning in my broadcasting history when, with the help of John Joyce on Outside Broadcasts and with the tacit encouragement of my editor, who snored quietly in the little shed behind me, I felt proud to be Irish and a broadcaster with RTE.

Highways and Byways had become a national icon and I was swept along with it. Invitations to visit events and people poured in like, for example, a call to visit Tullyvin to record there the happenings in Nobby Clarke's Pub. This turned out to become an extraordinary event. Peter Smith and Mickey Brady ensured that I arrived safe and relatively sound in the heart of county Cavan and like many another occasion on *Highways and Byways* it happened late at night. Bill O'Donovan, Head of 2FM, a man immersed in the national lore was there with Lucia Proctor, so RTE was well represented.

Nobby and Mrs Clarke were busy. Between ministering to a full house – it was now approaching midnight – and tending to their fish supper, they took the time to invite me in and to introduce me to the local Garda sergeant and Cavan legend Mick Higgins who was there with some of his men to ensure that law and order prevailed and that the story of the All-Ireland Final in New York in 1947 was well-told. By the way, there wasn't a Kerryman in sight. Tony Tighe was also present as was Gene Stuart, the country singer who was in no way perturbed when called, 'come on Gene sing your greatest hit, "Lovely Leitrim"!'

By now it was approaching late night to early morning and Nobby was emotional. 'You saw that monument to the boys who died for freedom as you came in', he asked. There was respectful silence with a few whispers of 'Lord have mercy on the dead', as he told his story. This concerned a volunteer in the troubles who died, 'died in my arms', said Nobby, 'and as he went to meet his maker he turned and said 'fight on Nobby, I'm fucked'. A man in the corner sang 'The Hackler from Grousehall', a local huntsman emerged with three beagles and sounded a hunting horn as I headed for Dublin and that day's edition of *Highways and Byways*.

Another night with Bill O'Donovan found us in Granard, Co. Longford where we were welcomed by Larry and 'Big Dan', Tommy Kiernan, sadly no longer with us. I made recordings here, there and everywhere and was amazed when a man brought in a uniform which had been worn by General Sean McKeon, the renowned 'Blacksmith of Ballindee' when we all visited the local hotel where Kitty Kiernan, Michael Collins' fiancée once lived. Songs were sung and tales were told as James Macken and his son, the great horseman Eddie, were among those to fill the tapes of *Highways and Byways*. The evening concluded in the pub of P. King, a name thought by many to refer to the great city in China. Peking!

I was not surprised to be welcomed thus, 'you're a Corkman sir, wearing the red of the rebels, you're one of our own in the capital of Red China'. I thanked him.

The programme had taken over my life. Days were spent recording in studio and nights recording and travelling throughout the country. I embarked on many strange and wonderful journeys in pursuit of stories. Among the most unusual was my journey to Buenos Aires with the Aer Lingus hurling team. There was even talk that I might play! Fortunately for everyone I never did but I certainly brought back the stories.

The Hurling Club of Buenos Aires was central to our plans and the late John Scanlon, Limerick born, set up the amazing sequence of events that followed. I met the Irish many of whose families were there since after the famine when Fr Fahy, a great Dominican, brought many out from the midlands in Ireland, men first and women later to marry and settle down in the land of the Pampas. The Misses Fox surprised me with undiluted Irish accents, although Sally Rattigan did not, she came from Wexford and married Johnny, a born Argentinian. Br John Burke, a north Corkman whose late mother I got to know very well, was then Principal in Newman College. Apart from being 'one of our own', he was a fine hurler. One of his confreres, Br O'Brien was from Co. Limerick and he introduced me to a priest of the Passionist order who brought me to a scene of vile murder where some young Passionists were despatched as they watched television. The room has remained untouched and is a cold disturbing place.

While I was there I visited a German who described graphically the last days of the great battleship 'Graf Spec' and her heroic captain Langsdorf. Evita's grave and the wonderful River Plate football stadium were inevitable ports of call. Diego Maradona was playing that night and I can remember the whispers growing to roars that greeted his every move: 'Maradona, Maradona, Maradona' echoed around the stadium. John Scanlon brought me with him and I sat in the commentator's boxes and met their famous broadcaster who utters an enlongated 'G-O-A-L' when they score.

There was a televised press conference afterwards and I was invited to put a question to their Bogartesque manager who sat elegantly smoking with his coat draped across his shoulders. I tried 'Do you think that Liam Brady is as good a player as Diego Maradona?'

He looked quizzically at me through a haze of his smoke, and smilingly replied, 'ah Irelandese, you are welcome, sometimes I like to make a joke too!' His smile hardly reached his eyes. I asked no more questions.

Our Sunday was spent on the Great Pampas where magnificent Argentine beef was barbecued. Mass was said by Fr Fidelis Rush who talked to me of Tang, reciting with affection: 'In leafy Tang the wild birds sang' and reminding me that William Bulfin had been editor of *The Southern Cross* which I receive regularly from Argentina. Somebody else remembered the words of Leo Casey's immortal 'Rising of the Moon'.

> Oh thank God, there still are beating
> Hearts in manhoods' burning noon,
> Who would follow in their footsteps
> At the rising of the moon.

Nowadays, whenever I meet Mary B. Murphy of the Irish Argentine Society or my two colleagues Bill Meek or Seamus Hosey I long to return there.

Highways and Byways took me to Lebanon in the pre-Christmas days of 1978. I flew into Tel Aviv and was subsequently refused entry into Lebanon by the Israeli Border Security. I spent a frustrating time in northern Israel in a hotel mistakenly called 'The Garden of Eden' before taking a taxi to Jerusalem where I met General Bill Callaghan, then UN Supremo. He brought me to Mass in a Nuns' Hospital where it was extraordinary to look out the window and see the biblical landscape unfold before your eyes.

I made my journey to Beirut by Cyprus and spent a happy evening there with Col. Tom Waters and his men. The flight into the shattered and war-mangled city of Beirut was spectacular although the tension at the airport was palpable. I was most relieved to see the blue berets of the UN and to travel with them to Tibnin, Camp Shamrock in Southern Lebanon.

Col. Vincent Savino, who was officer commanding made me, the first broadcaster from RTE to record greetings from the troops, heartily welcome as did all his staff. I was taken everywhere in the region and recorded messages and greetings in the most unlikely places. 'War torn', 'bravery under fire', and 'bomb disposal' took on a totally new meaning. Commdt Barry O'Sullivan introduced me to the bizarre and lethal world of bomb disposal where courage and humour fused (if that's a good word) and a perilous job was done without fuss or undue excitement. I came away most impressed with our army and, yet again, proud to be Irish.

There is a torrid postscript to this first visit to the Irish Army in the Lebanon. I brought home a bottle of arak which is an alcohol distilled from coco sap or rice and which comes from the Arabic word for 'sweat' or 'arak al tamr' – 'alcoholic spirit from dates'. Anyway, lethal describes it. On the day of our Christmas party I poured it into a bowl. John Skehan, who had just returned from Poland, added a bottle of 'pure Polish vodka', while Padraic Dolan, after a less spectacular journey to the West, dropped into all this concoction a bottle of real 'uisce beatha'. This was a night that a colleague temporarily mislaid his teeth and Diarmuid O Muirithe invited me to take part in an Irish language broadcast dealing with Christmas customs. What with jet lag from my journeys, I very sensibly felt unable to take part in the programme! The following day was not pleasant!

* * *

The third Sunday in September 1973 marked new and distinctive departures for *Highways and Byways*. This was the day when I returned to my roots in a way that would soon colour much of my broadcasting. My career for some time had been closely bound up with the world of arts, folklore and local history and now I was about to add to all this the wide-ranging world of the GAA. This would mark in many ways a return to my boyhood dreams and emotions.

I was sitting at home watching Cork footballers win the All-Ireland football title in Croke Park, thinking vaguely that the last time they had done was in 1945, I had listened to Michael O'Hehir on the wireless. Names flooded in: Tadhg Crowley, the Captain, Derry Beckett, Jack Lynch, Eamon Young, Mick Tubridy, Caleb Crone and many others from the past joined the new world of Jimmy Barry Murphy, Ray Cummins and the Captain, Billy Morgan. It was, in fact Billy's speech in Croke Park that made me load my tape machine, and with my very young children on board, drive to their hotel and meet many of the team and County Secretary, Frank Murphy in their hotel.

People and their places were always the cherished backbone of *Highways and Byways*. These led me down new ways to the world of local pride. Through RTE and my recordings there were few places in Ireland not presented with warm positive opportunities to bestow their dreams and their achievements on listeners. Every parish, every townland had a story to tell. Everyone could be on *Highways and Byways*.

I'm reminded of a lovely day in Thurles when Taoiseach Jack Lynch discussed with me in his analytical way a hurling match between Cork and Clare and then passed me on to President Paddy Hillery for a slightly sadder analysis. Cork always beat Clare then! On my way to the sideline I met Dermot Halpin from Newmarket-on-Fergus who was gazing in his mind's eye towards the mystic and romantic hurling strongholds of east Clare. 'Listen boy,' he said,

> you know Clare were never beaten. The shadows of Tul Considine, 'Goggles' Doyle and Jimmy Smith, all of whom you know, will lead us yet! We'll leave behind us the world of Biddy Early and some fine day in September, the heroes from Clare will bring McCarthy back to the banner.

He was now in full flight and turned impassioned to Denis Conroy, the great man from Carrigtwohill, and said 'oh God, wouldn't you die happy to see Clare winning an All-Ireland'. Conroy looked at Halpin, then at the *Highways* microphone and said, 'Christ, Dermot if that's the case you'll live forever!' On that day Cork went on to garner the usual result. The man of the match was Ger Loughnane ... was Biddy's curse fading and was the spirit of Brian Boru stirring?

By this time I had began recording material in Croke Park on big match days and I have vivid memories of the All-Ireland Final between the hurlers of Cork and Wexford in 1977. This was joy. My two favourite hurling counties in full flow, my tape machine ready for action and the great stadium was mine! I roamed the sidelines, talking here, recording there and reflecting as best I could the great atmosphere.

Tony Doran, Mick Butler, the Quigley brothers for Wexford and Martin Coleman, Martin O'Doherty, Sean O'Leary, Charlie McCarthy,

Jimmy Barry-Murphy and many others carried the hopes and dreams of the rebels and the yellow bellies as I, lucky man, recorded my story for *Highways and Byways*. Lucky Donncha! I always won. I supposed I was somewhat before my time, recording atmosphere, describing the scene and talking to fans.

Dungiven in Co. Derry was another home from home for *Highways and Byways*. Ann Brolly, of whom you'll hear more later, invited me up for a recording and through her husband, Francie, I met Liam Hemphy, a Kilkenny man whose love of Dungiven and Francie's sister, whom he married, was as large as his love of hurling. The children were very small when I first met them but I well remember Joe Brolly, the most famous Derry footballer of his generation. Of course I would say that.

Anyway, some years later, I was walking down the sideline in Croke Park on All-Ireland day when I was hailed by a child's voice, a young voice of certainties. 'Hello', he called from the Hogan Stand. I stopped and looked up. 'I'd like to come down to the sideline', he said. And I said to this chirpy little fellow, 'who are you anyway?' 'I'm Brolly from Dungiven, I'm Joe!' Before I could say anything, helpful hands were passing down across the wire, still talking. 'You know Ann and Francie Brolly, you stayed in our house'. Say no more. We walked around by the Canal end. He was looking at everything. 'Will you be passing the Kerry dug out ', he asked. I would and why did he want to know. 'I'd like to watch the match from there,' he said. A friendly Kerry mentor gave the nod and as I left I heard him introducing himself to the men of the kingdom.

That was Joe Brolly's first appearance in Croke Park and I am very proud of it. I often marvel at his lethal skills and speed, taken, perhaps, by osmosis from Pat Spillane! I do not know where he learned to blow kisses to the crowd. I must ask Ann and Francie.

By the early 1980s, I had acquired a small chair on which I sat in between action in Croke Park, taking care never to sit in front of the advertising hoardings. I was instructed never to 'obscure our advertisers'! I'm seated in front of the canal on the first Sunday in September in 1981 reflecting the tricolour colours of the Offaly hurlers and the more conservative maroon of Galway. It's approaching half-time and it looks as if the men from the West are on their way to victory while the throng from the faithful county will return home empty handed. A bag-carrying Ossie Bennett, the physio, tells me, 'we'll have them in the second-half'. He was 'rubbing' for Offaly.

During the half time I pressed on with recording of the game. A small boy in an Offaly cap asked, 'may I talk to your programme?' No doubt.

Everyone talks on *Highways and Byways*! A rhetorical question. 'Who will win?' The reply was distinct even in a babble of sound. 'Offaly, of course'. I could not resist, 'I'll be in Lourdes tomorrow there will be a miracle there too'. Great applause from those all around.

Offaly won. A mixture of Johnny Flaherty magic, Damien Martin courage, flare and skill from the late Pat Carroll, calmness under pressure from Pat Fleury, never mind the raking pucks of Pat Delaney who a few years later sang 'The Offaly Rover' for me in his home, or the flashing black helmet of Joachim Kelly. All the great Connollys and their lionhearted friends crossed the Shannon empty-handed.

There is a postscript. Later that Sunday night I arrived uninvited, but heartily welcome to the Offaly celebrations in the Gresham Hotel. Liam Fleury introduced me to Br Denis, a north Cork man, now naturalised in Offaly who has wrought wonders in school and adult hurling in Birr. He invited me down to Tullamore to meet the hurlers the following evening. The *Highways* tape machine worked overtime and to my great delight I was introduced with the team to a great hurling throng, and as I took my bow, I heard a voice distinctly say: 'Aha, you Cork man, we won and you didn't have to go to Lourdes!' Indeed, yes, everyone listened to *Highways and Byways*!

The GAA training pitch in Belfield in the university grounds in Dublin was where I relaxed and played all-star hurling with my four young lads Feargal, Ruairi, Donal and Donncha. On certain evenings, however, we stopped to watch the energetic training of members of the great Kerry team. Here it was that Jack O'Shea and Co. answered every call of their Dublin trainer, Mícheál O'Muircheartaigh. One evening as dusk approached we continued our puck around. A flying sliotar clipped the edge of my glasses, off flew the lens, and that was how a wonderful bunch of Kerrymen went on their knees for a Corkman. As Mícheál said 'an unlikely happening Donncha, especially on Munster Final Day!' They also found the lens.

Ger Power was one of the great and friendliest Kerrymen of his generation. I travelled down to Tralee to record a programme with him. Like the Rings in Cloyne, his room was a shrine to our native games. Mrs Power made the tea and Ger casually introduced me to his father whom I had never noticed until then. The penny dropped. This was the great Jackie Power of Ahane and Limerick fame. I checked my tapes, three always carried, three filled *Highways and Byways*. There was little left for Ger when I finished with Jackie!

I first grew to know and appreciate the work of Comhaltas Ceoltóirí Eireann through the friendship and hospitality of Labhrás O Murchu and his wife Una. I attended and recorded part of their summer entertainment seisúin for *Highways and Byways* and Labhrás asked, completely unexpectedly on my part, if I would like to write and present one of their North American Tour Shows. Would I what? Thereby began one of my greatest contretemps with RTE, one which left me, and certainly middle-management, with wounds that have never healed.

The fact that I left without informing anyone speaks volumes in itself and may well have merited the words 'gross dereliction of duty through *ultra vires* behaviour', but certainly did not merit the words 'you usurped the function of the editor of *Three-O-One*'. There was no such programme at the time! Or that 'you exceeded your authority', which is the biggest joke of all seeing that I had generally, during my *Highways and Byways* days, recorded on my own, early and late and without either assistance or direction.

In fact, material to cover the period of my proposed absence had been recorded by me on the weekend prior to my departure. It was transferred to Dublin for the attention of the editor of *Highways and Byways*, all properly linked and arranged. It was then found not to be suitable, perhaps, because 'you made these recordings privately on portable equipment without regard for RTE's standards'. Anyway, when the dust and a modicum of bad-humoured codology had settled, all the material recorded by me during my *ultra vires* days was transmitted as it was to the great joy and satisfaction of my editor and myself!

On the two following years when I went on Comhaltas tours, I informed RTE of my intentions and suffered no further angst. From a distance of years I regret what happened. Mea culpa, mea culpa, mea maxima culpa.

The tour parties included many of the greatest performers in the land including Joe Burke, a very young Paddy Glackin, Ann Mulqueen, Ann Brolly, Seamus MacMathuna, Donncha O Muineacháin, Celine Hession, Mona Lennon, Seamus Connolly, Donal de Barra, the Siamsa Céili Band and Gabriel McKeon, Seamus O'Dufaigh, Denis Ryan and many other splendid artistes. The two tour managers I remember are both sadly now longer with us, Diarmuid O Caithan whose great cry, 'there'll be no emblems worn on stage', with a less than covert look in my direction, and the gentle Tom Glackin.

The Fleadhanna Ceoil in Buncrana remain firmly fixed in my mind. They were among my first Fleadh recordings and John McCracken's organisational skills make easy the hurried life of a broadcaster. There is no doubt, too, that the sessions in the Piper's Club in Thomas Street in Dublin were unique.

They were my first sample of traditional Irish music and can never be forgotten, not only for the music, the friendliness and the atmosphere of this curiously tatty place, but for the host or fear a'tí, Jim Nolan. Jim was noted for his somewhat eccentric introductions of guests which were among the most endearing aspects of the Club. It is said that he once introduced Sean Connery as 'Mr O'Connor, I think'. Ulick O'Connor, a regular guest, caused Jim no little confusion. 'Ulick' became confused with 'Eunuch', or so they said. I got the full treatment, 'ladies and gentlemen, we have a very famous man from the radio here this evening ... pausing he leaned towards me, 'what's your name please?' And then raising his voice he declaimed, 'Mr Donaki O'Donaki', I have heard worse.

I became great friends with Jim who came on one of the American tours and when we were sharing a room in a large and expensive pad, he remarked cheerfully, 'this is a lovely little house ye have although I'd say it might be a bit cold in the winter'.

Our hostess was speechless, but she bravely carried on. 'What would all you folks like for breakfast, a large one I suppose?' which I thought was somewhat rhetorical.

Jim was undaunted. 'Whatever is handy, mam, and a nice bit of fried bread. By the way I'd like to sleep next to the wall.'

Our host, like all the kind and generous people who shared their homes with us, was phlegmatically and stolidly concise. 'Yes sir, yes indeed', he seemed to say to me, 'very existentialist'. Maybe he had never heard of 'fried bread' but Jim Nolan certainly had it for his breakfast.

The American experience is one that I cherish. The Gannons in St Louis stand out among my friends. PJ, whose mouth organ slow-airs have often been heard on radio while Helen's hospitality and splendid efficiency are bywords among the Irish in America. The Comhaltas, both here and there, are well deserving of the nation's gratitude. Without my Comhaltas experiences my *Highways and Byways* might have been poorer and my life might have lost the real riches of Ireland.

Many and many a night was spent recording music and talking with the greats of Irish music. I am reminded now of Leo Carty's lilting and storytelling in Broadway, Co. Wexford, Paddy Parle leading his mummers and Paddy Berry singing 'Ballyshannon Lane' on a great night of Comhaltas music.

CHRISTY RING:
The Cuchulainn of Cloyne

Walking past the dug-outs in Croke Park was like appearing before a who's who of hurling greats – Christy Ring, Fr Bertie Troy, Denis Conroy, Frank Murphy and Jimmy Brohan sat forward in excitement, while the late Garda Tom Troy, once a famous boxer, but now every inch an exile Corkman sat on the edge of the hurling 'holy of holies'. I caught Ring's eye and he smiled. Twas like wearing the red jersey! Derry Gowan from Fermoy, always a kindly man, asked if I would like to meet the team later. Would I what!

As it happens, later was much later. It was in fact early the following morning when I entered the Cork team hotel. As I stepped into the lift, a voice said, 'hold it please'. It was Christy Ring. Now I knew that he was not much given to casual chat, so I was wary. He looked at me with piercing blue eyes. 'Didn't I see you yesterday? What are you doing here? I often listen to your *Highways and Byways* when I'm travelling.' I told him my mission, a few words with the Cork team. He lit up, 'I'll help you'.

I tried, 'would you talk?' He would and within minutes I was in his room.

'Where will we start?' he asked.

I said, '1954, I was at it, the year you won your eighth All Ireland Medal'.

He sat on the edge of the bed and remembered.

> There was that great man Jim English and what would you say about the Rackards, great friends, too, even in '56 when Foley saved one! They were nature's gentlemen, big, strong and skilful. No wonder they did us proud in '98.' I was astounded. This was real stream of consciousness radio. 'There's nothing you couldn't do with the hurley ... heart and skill – that's what's needed.

That was my first real meeting with the great Christy Ring. Others were recorded with him in the family home in Cloyne, magic moments captured for radio, and for television too. His friend Willie John Daly said to me once, 'there was no one like Ring and there never will be another'. How right he was. And I never wrote the book!

Early memories of Christy are linked with the folklore of Pairc Ui Chaoimh and Denis Conroy's incredible love for the place and the game: Denis telling stories of cycling to Thurles during the war years with his tyres filled with hay or Willie John Daly remembering travelling to matches with Christy driving and Mattie Fouhy's mother sprinkling them with holy water on their way, or Denis, again holding up a fistful of grass in Pairc Ui Chaoimh and saying, 'there's blood and history and hurling tradition in every blade of grass in this place'.

I taped himself and Christy sitting on an empty stand in the Park: Denis dropping the God-names of his heroes like snuff at a wake or Christy, silent, intense and locked in his own thoughts unless you mentioned Cloyne and then his old mentor Gerry Moynihan would spring to his lips, or the Glen and he would talk of Youngie or Paddy O'Donovan or indeed, Tommy Doyle or Seán Herbert. Jim Young and Paddy O'Donovan were great stalwarts of Glen Rovers, while Tommy Doyle and Seán Herbert starred for Tipperary and Limerick respectively. I was so lucky to be admitted into this select company, so happy to record them all for *Highways and Byways*. Let me not forget Fr Bertie Troy, now Canon Troy, it was he who set up Christy and me for two memorable interviews.

I was privileged, too, to welcome Christy as a guest to my home on an All-Ireland eve. He brought with him two of the stars of the Cork team, Dermot McCurtain and Tom Cashman. He held forth at length on the importance of good food for the young hurlers and insisted, while all the rest of us ate rolls and sweet cake, that they both ate fresh ham and travelled back early to their hotel. He looked affectionately after them and before he left shook the hand of my son Donal who was then a juvenile dual player with Kilmacud Crokes. Ring looked him in the eye and said, 'Donal, young fellow, always remember tonight, a great night and who you met in your home'. Derry Gowan smiled. What we would all remember was Christy himself and our briefly touching greatness on the night before an All-Ireland.

* * *

The very last time that I spoke to Christy Ring we were in Cloyne. 'It was here', he said, 'it all started.' That was less than a month before his untimely death in 1979. Much of this came back to me during the recent re-run of *Highways and Byways* on RTE Radio 1. I thought this book was finished but memories drew me back to the little village of Cloyne in east Cork and back to my hurling hero who lies at rest in his native place.

To chronicle a few events in his life story: Christy Ring was born on 12 October 1920, the fourth child of Nicholas and Mary. This blonde child, reared in the famed surroundings of a well-preserved Round Tower, with echoes of St Colman and the founding of the see of Cloyne in the sixth century, was to become even more famous than at least two others who had associations with his native place. Bishop Berkeley, the eighteenth-century philosopher lived here for some years and here, too, was born William Maxwell Kenneally, who is best remembered for his famous ballad 'The Moon Behind the Hill'. Christy was born, too, in a year which witnessed the killings of the two Lord Mayors of Cork, Tomás MacCurtain and Terence MacSwiney. It was the year, too, of 'Bloody Sunday' and of the 'Boys of Kilmichael', not to mention, much nearer to home, an attack by the volunteers on Cloyne barracks.

Back in 1979, I talked to Paddy Motherway, one of Christy's school mates in the early years of boyhood.

> We played endless matches in what is now Cloyne Cemetery. We used coats for goalposts, and Christy, the smallest of us all stood between the goalposts. We had no watches, no referees. Usually it was whichever team scored twelve goals first was the winner. We stopped at dusk.

> Christy stopped everything he could reach. He had no fear. He was full of courage. He was always where the ball was. You'd see his fair head everywhere.

Christy carried his hurley everywhere with him and many a long summer evening was spent 'shooting' at the local coal store. He would stand back some thirty yards and drive the ball unerringly at a particular shutter which was less than a foot in width. He rarely missed. To prove a point to any friendly sceptics he dipped his rubber ball in a bucket of water before shooting and, so, the point of impact was always visible on the shutter.

I remember well calling into the National School in Saleen to meet the late Gerry Moynihan who had been one of the early Ring mentors. Gerry never had any doubts.

> I was watching the youngsters pucking around and immediately spotted Christy. His determination was unique. I organised a street league. Christy was about thirteen at the time. He never believed in being on a losing side and was, of course, the star of his street.

Gerry invited me home to his house in Cloyne and talked on until dusk turned into night and Mrs Moynihan had made the tea and the fire glowed in the grate, glowed and flamed, indeed, like Gerry's memories.

He then made the most profound remark ever made about Christy Ring. 'It would have been a greater achievement to stop him being a hurler than to make a hurler of him.'

When I mentioned Gerry's remarks to Christy, he just smiled and said in his modest way, 'Cloyne was always very good to me. I just played for the love of the game. I'll never forget that old school. I always loved hurling in Cloyne.'

I talked to Christy of many matches and he always returned to the Munster Hurling Championship and he fired my enthusiasm and re-kindled my memories to a flaming day in Limerick in 1949 when I saw my first inter-county hurling match. It was a day of Cork – Tipperary size when sun and sky and hurling conjoined in ensuring that day in the Limerick Gaelic grounds would be forever deep in the heart's core. It was my first time hearing Tipperary accents and seeing the long, sleek motor cars transporting our heroes in whispering elegance to the Eamhain Macha of dreams. Red and white and blue and gold coalesced in friendly rivalry. The old programme is tattered, but, even now, the names – T. Reddan, P. Stakelum, J. Devitt, T. Doyle, P. Shanahan, Sonny Maher, T. Mulcahy, W. Murphy, A. Lotty, J. Lynch, W. J. Daly and C. Ring – tick like time-bombs in the corners of memory. Christy Ring – twas like a silent roar from the heart!

They always said – 'Toscanini for the opera, Kathy Barry for the crubeens and Ringy for the goals. Cork and Tipp you can't, you'll never, beat them.' This was heart-thumping stuff and I was trying to see where Michael O'Hehir wove his verbal symphonies. What were they thinking of? Thirty years later, the late and wonderful Tommy Doyle told me:

> Paddy Leahy brought me into Sadliers Hotel, minutes before we went to the game. 'You'll be marking Christy Ring,' he said. 'That's the man we have to beat.' I listened and I knew. Twas a different thing then. The talking was over and then you see a man like Ring coming towards you and the flags waving and the terrible noise. That was it. No peace when you're marking Ringy – and very little talking.

The Ring versus Doyle language was spoken with hurleys in fierce hip-to-hip communication and bone-to-bone endeavour. Tommy was most successful in the 1949 encounter and received a strange letter from a Limerick hurler: 'could you please write down the way to mark Christy Ring?'

Tommy summed it up for me. 'You could write down some things but no two pages would be the same. The script was always changing. He was always watching for the smallest chance, always lurking towards the edge of the square.'

Another great Doyle, John from Holy Cross, holder of eight All-Ireland medals himself, understood. 'What Ring did with a hurley on the edge of a square was what made hurling the great game it used to be.'

My first visit to Limerick ended in stalemate. 34,702 fans paid at the gate and I was one of them. Tipp won the replay and I was not there. I was making hay in east Cork!

It was 1951 before I next saw Cork and Tipperary in action. Pat Stakelum reminded me of Ring. 'He was always moving, non-stop, poetry in motion, you never knew what he'd do next. He could change a whole game with a flick of his wrist.' Cork lost, but to many of us in the huge attendance in Limerick, and to the thousands who were locked out and listening outside, the day belonged to Ring. Playing at midfield, minus boots and socks, he waged his own little battle against the might and wiles of the Munster Champions. I think it was his finest hour, but, of course, we could not know what still lay ahead. Pat Stakelum summed it up, 'there was only one Ring.'

Our day came soon. It was on Sunday 13 July when Ring, and Cork, at last wrestled the Munster crown from Tipperary. It was Cork's first drift towards the magical three in a row. The papers clarioned, 'Cork defy Tipperary effort to save hurling crown.' 40,000 of us saw it happen and Ring's second-half performance drew the usual superlatives.

Another year had passed and once again the old rivals faced each other in Limerick. Once again the papers told the story. 'Ring's first minute put Cork on road to 27th title'. Cork 3-10 Limerick 1-11. Christy, the captain was unstoppable. He scored one goal and eight points, an incredible feat in the face of the tightest, most skilful and toughest defence in the land. John D. Hickey writing in the *Irish Independent* accorded a classical and prophetic accolade. 'A year from now, I venture to suggest that the only vivid recollection of the hour will be the almost incredible artistry of the greatest hurler of them all, the one and only Christy Ring.'

He was right! 52,449 of us crowded into Limerick on a July day to see Cork take their 'three in a row' as Christy marched towards his eighth All-Ireland medal. Every time he even touched the ball, the Cork fans chanted, 'Into the kitchen Ringy Boy?' He invariably obeyed. That was the year that Christy's friend, the late Bryan MacMahon, penned his immortal tribute.

> How oft I've watched him from the hill move here and there in grace,
> In Cork, Killarney, Thurles town or by the Shannon's Race;
> Now Cork is bet, the hay is saved, the thousands wildly sing,
> They speak too soon, my sweet garsún for here comes Christy Ring.

Jimmy Magee, writing in the *Sunday World* on 4 March 1979, paid his tribute to Christy: 'Christy Ring, I thought would live forever and somehow he will as a lasting legend that will prosper as long as men respect greatness.'

It's difficult to leave Christy. Let us have a last memory provided by the generous and kindly man from Drumcollogher, Donie Broderick. It tells the story of how Ring 'foxed Mackey's greyhounds' in Thurles in 1956. Donie, a strong and unyielding hurler was entrusted with Ring! He takes up the tale,

> Ring changed a whole match and destroyed the Limerick team. In the days before the game, the build-up was typically Munster, training, talking and encouragement from the great Mick Mackey.

During the game, Donie was hurling well within himself and actually enjoying his assignment:

> I was doing quite well and we had several tussles, very fair but very hard. Before half-time we were well on top. I, a corner back, was 70 yards out, clearing a ball down the field to Vivion Cobbe, who scored a lovely point. There was a mighty cheer and it felt like victory. In the second half, twas much the same. Ring was quiet, too quiet with hindsight. As I think of it now, I think we were lulled into a false sense of security, and, then, with the match in the bag, Ring burst the bubble.

> He seemed agitated and began to move around and ran to the sideline and came back like a man with a mission, now he went into the centre-forward position and I was marking Josie Hartnett. Tension was everywhere. Ring was like a tiger and then, before I knew it there was another change and he was back in the corner. Things began to happen. Ringy seemed to explode again and again, goal followed goal, point followed point and we were broken. He seemed like a man on fire and even ran behind the goal to raise the green flag himself. You couldn't really watch him.

Donie Broderick was right. Ring was exalted and the Cork team with him. A fine young Limerick team was crushed. The man from Drumcollogher was philosophical, 'No matter how or where you played with Christy, he'd make you famous .... Three goals and more that day and they remember me! He does, too, and often called in to see me at home.' I remember, too, I spoke to Mick Mackey about it. He was cryptically but not grudgingly appreciative of Ring. 'That's genius.' he said, 'and you know what that is.' Mick, while he didn't say it had more than a few grains of genius himself. He knew!

I met Jimmy Smyth, the first class player in Croke Park a few Sundays ago. I was reminded of another day with Ring on Munster's teams. He said, 'He was a hurler's hurler, fearless in the field, even when he wasn't brilliant, he was great. he was the greatest.' It's worth remembering that he won 18 Railway Cup medals with Munster and, in the process, scored 42 goals and 105 points. The greatest.

Pat Fanning, from Waterford, summed it up. 'There was only one Christy Ring. Not alone did he embody the spirit of hurling, he became the very sport itself. We need another Christy Ring.'

My television interview with Christy in Cloyne marked a green flag in my own broadcasting life. It was a compelling and quite extraordinary experience that I will never forget. I never knew when he shook my hand that I would never see him again. When the interview was over, he smiled and walked away. Canon Bertie Troy, then a curate in Ballycotton, Derry Gowen, Frank Murphy and the unforgettable Denis Conroy remain inextricably linked to that moment.

The Ring legend enfolded me. His last words before the interview remain fresh: 'Please make sure that Rita and the kids are included in the programme. This is their day too.' And then, of course, the words that seemed to offend so many: 'You'll write the book', a statement of fact made to me by Christy himself. I never had any ambitions to go into print. Radio was my medium, but he asked. No one can deny that. Maybe the time is ripe – 'beidh laetheanta eile'.

I was listening to Christy on tape the other day and was struck by his humour, sardonic and often rueful. He was remembering the 1946 All-Ireland Final against Kilkenny. 'Cork in 1946 was,' he suggested,

> the greatest of them all ... everything went well that day. I always remember a funny incident ... Now, it was one of the best games I'd ever played, but early on I missed two scoreable frees and I always remember coming out of the gate of Croke Park when a spectator, a friend of mine, said, 'By God, you played a great game but, how did you miss the first two frees?

Ring smiled to himself at the demands of friend and foe alike and this triggered off another memory, 'another day in Croke Park ... and one of our centre-field men, Seán Barrett of Kinsale had played a marvellous game.' Christy reminded us that Seán was, as they say, getting on at the time and the ubiquitous and all-demanding spectator was heard to say, 'Barrett played a marvellous game today. He should retire now!'

Later on in our conversation, Christy summed up the achievement of playing for Cork.

> I arrived in Killarney for the All-Ireland Minor Hurling Final in 1937 wearing a No. 26 jersey and from that day until I retired I was never without a Cork jersey in some grade. I played in 1938 (minor), played junior in 1939 and then played senior for Cork in 1940 and from then until the day I retired I was on both Munster Railway Cup and Cork senior hurling teams.

Before we finished our long conversation, he made his celebrated remark about Tipperary hurlers, 'I suppose they are Cork's greatest rivals and, without Tipp, the GAA is only half-dressed. They're our greatest rivals and our greatest friends.'

Finally, I asked him the ultimate and leading question: 'Which was your last game?'

He looked me straight in the eye and, without pausing, said, 'I don't remember any game as being my last game.' Like his life, Christy never knew when it would end. There was no 'last game'.

Tim Lehane, one of my colleagues in RTE was recently stirred by the *Donncha's Highways Revisited* broadcasts. We were discussing Christy Ring when he showed a copy of a poem of Seán O Tuama's, reflective of my own thoughts

> Duirt bean os cionn a choirp ...
> Ba mhór an peaca é
> An fear san a adhlacadh.

Or, again, in Seán's words:

> Ní féidir liom-sa fós
> Christy Ring a adhlacadh ...
> Samhlaím é uaireannta ...
> sínte ar leac na honóra
> i mBrú na Bóinne.

Tim Lehane's own words are echoes of the originals:

> At his wake, a woman said ...
> What a cruel shame
> To bury such a man.

Tim continues:

> Myself, I'm not yet able
> to bury Christy Ring ...
> At times, I imagine him ...
> Stretched out on a slab of honour in Newgrange.

All that is left to me to say is again half-quote, half-aphoristic tribute.

'Ní fheicfear a leithéid arís.' We shall certainly never see his kind again, the Cuchulainn of Cloyne swinging his hurley like the young Setanta down the verdant years of all our memories. Weren't we lucky, those of us who saw him play, those of us who almost knew him.

Footsteps Into Time – Beginnings

'When the virus of restlessness begins to take possession of a wayward man, and the road from here seems broad and sweet, the victim must first find himself a good and sufficient reason for going'. These words, indicating as much of my 'virus of restlessness' as his own belong to John Steinbeck.

When his *Travels With Charley*, a tale of an odyssey across America with his dog, was first published, I was just about to begin my broadcasting career. It fired me with an extraordinary urge to see my own country and also to meet the writer. I did both. I met him, in the line of business, at around midnight on a frosty night in Waterville, Co. Kerry. It was January 1966. In my cold heaterless car I had a tape recorder, two books, *The Grapes Of Wrath* and *The Winter Of Our Discontent* and a dim and failing six-volt battery.

The night porter at the hotel was not exactly helpful. 'He's gone to bed sir', he said, adding 'Sir' almost as an afterthought.

'It was a long cold journey', I said. He softened, vanishing around the corner. He came back, looking worried. I wasn't surprised. Steinbeck materialised! He looked fierce and vaguely tousled. Tall, blackbearded, with grey-grizzly hair and wearing a dark red dressing gown, he might have been a less seedy version of 'Doc' in *Cannery Row*.

'I thought you might talk ...' I began.

'He's not giving interviews', an irate-looking lady spoke from behind his left shoulder.

'My wife's right', he said. 'What time of night is this to call?' It was obvious that no answer was expected.

I tried a usually successful ploy. 'I've come a long way' on rising inflection.

'That's as may be,' she said, not unkindly.

'I liked *Cannery Row*,' I said holding on.

'That was a long time ago in Monterey,' he said from the foot of the stairs.

No, there was no hope of an interview. I handed him the copies of *The Grapes Of Wrath* and *The Winter Of Our Discontent*. He looked surprised, and surprised me too when he invited me to meet him in the Metropole Hotel in Cork in a few days. He'd bring my books with him, autographed, and we would 'talk some'. We did. Had I ever been to Derry? No, not yet. His mother was of Derry stock while his father was German. 'We're travellers. Everyone should travel, get to feel your own country'. That long and seemingly pointless conversation with the Steinbecks has always remained with me. Everything else in my life has followed. When I was very young the urge to be someplace else was on me. Like Steinbeck, I have never improved. The disease was incurable. My journeys were all different; no two were alike. A new journey always discovered a new land.

I owe a great debt to Steinbeck and Charley for signposting the way. I owe much too, to one of my finest ever guests on radio, my Clare friend, Margaret Dooley who travelled to Dublin for the first time on her 101st birthday (she wasn't mightily impressed). Neither can I forget three neophyte travellers in their seventies who travelled with me to France on first passports!

Nothing surprised the late Jack Feery, Hippy Murphy and John McGinley. Except, perhaps when Jack observed, very accurately that 'They all talk very foreign over here!' As a result, Donncha's Holy Land Walk was probably dedicated to one woman, four men and a dog – all extraordinary travellers!

I always travelled to work, worked to travel. I loved my work. Travel and everything – literally everything – was incidental to it. Charity had no particular place in my busy working world.

Then, towards the end of 1981 when my radio programme *Highways and Byways* was at the peak of its national appeal and bringing me immense and joyful satisfaction, I decided quite without much foresight to 'give something back'. There was no blinding flash of light, no 'Road to Damascus', only an unreasoning and unexplainable need to give.

Some years earlier, Peter Stokes of the Irish Wheelchair Association had invited me to visit a 'Wheelchair' holiday in Co. Monaghan and it was here that I met handicapped people for the first time. It was around this time too, that I first met Frank Flannery and Stephen Farrelly of the

Rehabilitation Institute, when I was a recipient (to my great surprise) of some of their Entertainment Awards.

However, at this early stage I was content to sympathetically observe and to help through my *Highways and Byways*. In the autumn of 1981, I met Nick O'Hare, a specialist in Connemara ponies, at the RDS. He talked enthusiastically of his two favourites 'Let's Go' and 'Hullaballoo'. He invited me to join him for a short spin with either of the two under his smart gig. The hint of an idea was born. Why not a pre-Christmas fund-raising trip from Dublin to Cork? Nick was on! Before I left the RDS I phoned Peter Stokes. He was a bit surprised but delighted.

Dick Warner, producer of *Highways and Byways* was already booking 'lines'. Ted Berry, friend of many years and Outside Broadcast Unit guru would travel with us. Bishop Carroll of Dublin, Jim Ryan of Dunne's Stores, Sile de Valera and hundreds of others sent us off from Tallaght with blessings and good wishes. My travels for the handicapped had begun.

It snowed every day and 'Donncha's Highways and Byways Pony Trot' entered folklore. Everyone was generous. Even though I didn't know it at the time, I was bitten by the 'giving bug'!

Early the following summer, I walked from Bantry Bay to Ballycastle, Co. Antrim and broadcast 'live' on *Highways and Byways*. The Irish Wheelchair Association was again the beneficiary. I owe a great debt to All Ireland Champion walker Commdt Bernie O'Callaghan who had me trained to the ounce and to Osmond Bennett who always provided advice and the much-needed 'rub'. This was the best of all worlds for me, a happy coalescence of working and giving. That was the last summer of *Highways and Byways*, the last summer of a very happy phase of my life. Work was now reduced from a daily flood to a mere trickle.

Perhaps, I thought, I might be of some use to the handicapped. I was! I will always remember Hugh Coveney's words of comfort and encouragement when, as Lord Mayor of Cork and before the pictures of MacCurtain and MacSwiney in City Hall, he sent me on a new journey. I am glad too, that his first post-*Highways* walk ended in Carraigtwohill in Co. Cork where my dear friends Fr Dan Gould, John Healy, Kevin Hickey and the late Denis Conroy launched me through the byways and highways of east Cork. A snowy walk, including fasting for Concern for 48 hours, from Dublin to Galway brought pre-Christmas cheer to wheelchair people. Walks followed in Wexford, Offaly, Westmeath, Louth, Monaghan, Clare, Kildare, Carlow and Limerick.

The Gaelic Athletic Association celebrated its centenary in 1984 and for me the year was an occasion for triple celebration. I launched my *Donncha's Sunday* on Radio One to mark the preparations and celebrations in Thurles for the All-Ireland Hurling Finals in Semple Stadium. I also walked from Croke Park to the stadium in aid of 'Concern'.

I was beginning to earn for myself the title of Ireland's greatest pedestrian and set off on my way on the preceding Friday morning at 6.00 a.m. It was to be a non-stop walk through more byways than highways to reach Thurles around midday on Sunday.

A battle of endurance might be a good way to describe it. I remember walking through the dark towards Monasterevin on the Friday night, in a blaze of blinding light from cars and trucks and now and again silent pools of darkness as late night arrived.

The dawn on the Saturday was quite uninspiring and the day turned to rain. Fr Finucane joined me here and there offering encouragement. Late in the day Micheál O Muircheartaigh and Br Liam O Caithnia, author of *Scéal na hIománá* a history of hurling from its beginnings to 1884, stopped on their way to the match to support and greet.

Dusk came rain-filled in Co. Laois. We had tea in Abbeyleix and the great march paused for more sustenance in Ballycolla. Rathdowney reminded me of our first stop there on the pony and trap journey. I wondered how were Hullabaloo and Let's Go. My thoughts were becoming chaotic. Errill was reached by 2.00 a.m. I saw a curtain pulled and a few dogs barked while the pre-dawn wind rippled over sweat – like a hot and cold shower. No talking now. Just slog.

Fr Finucane joined me at the dawn and we wandered uneasily into silent Templemore. Mass, breakfast, a short rest and a great welcome from the Gardai are my memories. I looked at my watch. I had been walking for 48 hours non-stop. Pain, stiffness and exhaustion occupied me. I tried to remember last night's trudge and was vaguely aware of having met Dermot Kelly, the hurler, and others. But now, eight miles to go and best foot forward. I'm not sure how an energy surge engulfed my embattled body but it did and I reached Thurles at an unlikely speed!

Thurles on All-Ireland day was unique, excitement and celebrations were everywhere. The Bank of Ireland was open and welcoming. Jim Whitty almost poured a Paddy into my outstretched hand. It surged into the deepest recesses of my body and spirit – uisce beatha indeed.

My father in the early 1930s.

Donncha on 'that' pony, while sister Kitty prepares to urge movement!

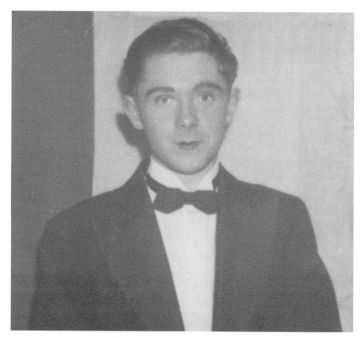

Donncha on stage in Charleville in 1954. Note make-up!

Donncha and Vera at the 'Guild Ball' UCC in 1960.

The family with Dev in 1966. Vera, Donal, Feargal, Sinéad, Donncha, Ruairí and of course, sean-Donncha!

Five of the same only later! Donal, Donncha, Feargal, Sinéad and Ruairí in celebratory mood at Feargal's wedding in 1998.

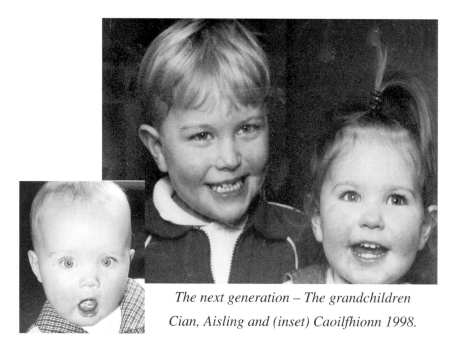

The next generation – The grandchildren
Cian, Aisling and (inset) Caoilfhionn 1998.

Marathon Monday 1984. Donncha and Donal 'speed' through the
Phoenix Park in Dublin.

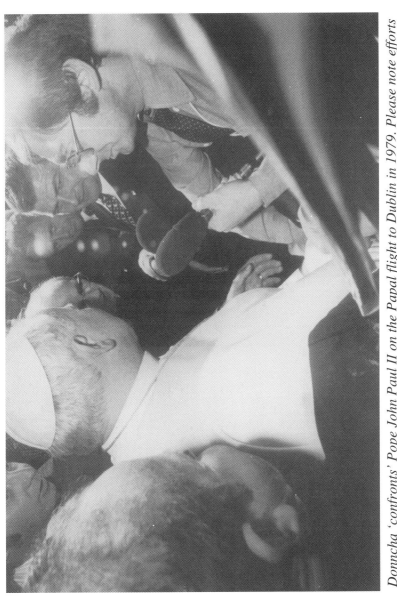

Donncha 'confronts' Pope John Paul II on the Papal flight to Dublin in 1979. Please note efforts of Archbishop Marcinkus to 'come between' the principals!

Donncha in a Napoleonic mode at Cahirmee horse fair in Buttevant. Donie O'Keeffe's horse is said to strongly resemble Napoleon's horse 'Marengo'. Donncha vaguely resembles himself!

Donncha meets Chaim Hertzog, President of Israel in 1985.

Donncha on the road to Jericho where he never fell among thieves!

Donncha on the Highways in Roscarbery, Co. Cork.
Forever facing towards Clonakilty.

Donncha and Sinéad on the epic Winter March in 1987 on the road from Glengarriff to Leitrim village in the footsteps of O Súilleabhaín Beara.

Donncha allegedly says slán at 65th birthday bash in RTE, acutely observed by Ronan Collins, Helen Shaw, Director of Radio, Bob Collins, Director General RTE, Judge Conor Maguire, Sen Labhrás O Murchú and Kathleen O'Connor, RTE.

But now I must begin again and walk to the game. Cork and Offaly were opponents and red and white and green, white and orange flags grew like flowers from every corner. My hand was pumped until I felt that it would fall off.

Finally, I reached my interview point with Jimmy Magee. I did my best, but disorientation had arrived full of unwelcome uncertainties and when I left him I had to ask for directions to the stand. It was ridiculous but here I was in Thurles, a place I knew so well and I couldn't remember anything! I had been walking for 55 hours without sleep and, indeed, I slept off and on, even falling off my seat, throughout the whole match which Cork won. All the ceremony and much of the excitement had passed me by. I was the only Corkman asleep when John Fenton took the McCarthy Cup! I finally got back to Dublin and bed around midnight. Nell McCarthy from Carraigtwohilll travelled with my family and myself. I could neither talk nor rest. I was still mentally walking when I hit the pillow. I had not slept for 66 hours. These were certainly my longest days.

Talking of long days, another stands out in 1984. It was the day that I have called 'Marathon Monday'.

Marathon Monday 1984

Most of the thousands of marathon runners who gathered on that cold morning in St Stephen's Green would have prepared assiduously for the greatest physical test of their lives. I was, as ever, blithely facing into a painful unknown. I rushed to the nearest tree, my third time this morning, it must be the nerves. Waking up this morning was like no other morning, a pint of hot water washed down with a sickening high concentrate of orange and honey and I was sick, noisily and nervously into the toilet bowl.

A man shook hands, 'good luck whatever' he said and he was gone. Other isolated and frightened souls flitted through the leaves shedding almost winter-like beauty on the Green and I made pin-pricking attempts to fasten on my race number. Donal, my son who would run with me seemed unconcerned. Isn't youth a strange thing? What did Shaw say? 'wasted on the young' – well I'm not sure. It would be his fourth marathon and he was 17. Not just that, he was in charge of money and keys. I have a tendency to lose both and to forget where cars are parked. Of course – he would take care of them, no problem –'have you got your headband he asked?' and he sauntered off through the loudspeaking marathon morning.

What the hell had I got myself into? I remember well the very first Dublin City Marathon standing at the gate of RTE in Nutley Lane and laughing long and loud at the speedsters and the stragglers as they came by in ever-diminishing numbers. They were the high steppers and the vast majority were limpers like I would be myself. I saw Ruairi Quinn and he didn't look too happy nor did several of my colleagues from RTE. Tom McGrane said to me, 'what do you think of that?' and I said, 'not much, a waste of time and muscle and anyway it should be Radio One and not Radio Two whose banner flies here'. Could I have guessed that by 1984 I would be among the myriads setting off in search of fulfilment. Anyway it was too late now to withdraw. Vanity rules.

A voice over the public address system was issuing peremptory instructions to Radio Two –'please take down your banner'. Radio Two was not answering. They were silent and unmoved and, anyway, without them there would have been very little publicity. We are soon making our way to Hatch Street, the morning was like my insides, doubtful. At a quarter to eleven the wheelchair contingent were on their way, next the elite ladies – please define an elite lady – surging over the first few yards of their marathon journey. Nervousness was everywhere, fear was palpable, sweaty palms were the order of marathon morning.

Ultan Macken fastened on to me like a leech. 'I've done lots of these', he said helpfully 'it is really quite intricate but alright if you know what you are doing', and he looked at his Radio Two watch. I hated him with an intensity difficult to measure and yet he was one of my friends. He whispered into my ear, 'don't take off too fast'. Good God, I'd be lucky to start at all, never mind finish.'How's your training?' he asked without a hint of sarcasm. I shut my ears.

It was all much too late. Why worry about something you never did then there were the jokes, the cat calls, the jeers, the cheers, the whistles, the pushes and the standing jogging. It would make you sick.

There's a wave from George Waters, the Director General. I wonder who'll be there this time next year. Directors General of RTE seem to come and go like the seasons but they always wave to you and smile which is a great consolation in your hour of need. Up there too I see Bill Wall, the controller of Radio Two, and I know that my friend Bill O'Donovan is waiting for me somewhere along the way, which sounds like a song only I'm in no mood for singing.

We're actually running, well half running. I can't remember seeing any clock, still it's all the same now. The pace is brisk enough. Along the South Circular Road people are clapping and waving and some are shouting 'mighty'. How did they know or even guess how good we were? There in the crowd I see my friend Helen Cole whose is married to Paddy, the jazz man, Helen is waving good luck. This must be the first feed station and the soon-to-be ubiquitous paper cups make their first appearance. I never touch a drop. I think longingly of a little tincture of poitín, how it would raise the spirits, stimulate the mind and deaden the fear.

Anyway, we cross Suir Bridge and we're into Bulfin Road. I try to lock into my own thoughts and remember William Bulfin and his beloved *Rambles in Eirinn,* a book which has had a considerable influence on my life and my thoughts flick away to a sunny day in the pampas of Argentina where all the talk was of Bulfin and his paper, the *Southern Cross.* Shuffle some more yards and we are here in Emmet Road.

When I'm in good form, I sing two verses and choruses of 'Bould Robert Emmet The Darling Of Eireann' which, incidentally, I once heard sung at the fair in Charleville as 'Bould Robert Emmet The Darliant Of Araiann' – no one running there and then we're into Grattan Crescent – the patriots are out in force this morning. There are that many running here, there will be several quorums for Grattan's Parliament. Did they run like this at the races of Castlebar, I wondered. I think I'm getting the flu.

Three miles gone and I'm feeling great, full of running but in a sinister corner of my mind, I know the score. Watch it, take it handy, there's a long road there yet. A handshake from Jim Tunney, TD is encouraging.

It's curiously silent in the middle of the multitude as I try to run towards the kerbside. Faces, like Cheshire cats materialise and then fade away. There is less banter now than there was at the start as we begin the long climb up Kylemore Road – I think I remember visiting Nora Connolly O'Brien up here somewhere to talk to her of 1916 and her late father, James Connolly. One runner near me stops. 'I'm fucked', he says. I understand and a dark shadow crosses my own and my neighbours' faces. By that first departure we too are reduced, finite. He was sitting on the kerb crying as we left him.

Colin Morrison, with whom I had shaken hands at the start was now running towards the middle of the road, his long legs beating like pistons and actually drawing away. 'It's lovely', he said – hardly my own feelings while Ultan was struggling somewhere behind. Donncha, you're paying for it now mate but there's a cheer and there's Tom Troy, decent Cork man and garda in Store Street. 'Up Cork' he says and catches my hand in a grip that would crush a gander. There are tears in my eyes from the handshake, 'good old Donncha' he shouts after me. The 'old' fits well today.

We're climbing the flyover and someone says 'two thirds are done' it's all downhill now. Liars. I hate that. They must be joking. I can't see Donal anywhere, I suppose like Colin his long legs are wafting him farther and farther away as I am left, as Keats might have said, 'alone and palely loitering'. There's Peter Stokes from the Irish Wheelchair Association. 'You're going great', he says. Did a Westmeath man ever tell the truth?

'Would you like a drink?' he asks. Not that kind, I think – still, Lucozade goes down well and a Mars Bar sinks powerfully into pallid and flaccid veins and I face the road for Raheny. More clapping but I don't give a damn. I'm going to finish this blasted marathon and suddenly Bill O'Donovan of Radio 2 with a delicate flower in his lapel, emerges from the multitude. 'Come into the van', he says and talk with Jimmy Greally. There too I see John Eames and I can't remember who else. Jimmy looks concerned . 'Are you bunched?' he says, 'you look a bit tired'. The crowd, several hundreds of them, cheer as he asks a rhetorical question, 'will you finish?' Will I what? Of course I will. Refusing a tea or a coffee I hasten up the hill like a demented hedgehog and the blasted rain comes down.

Eighteen miles have passed and I see Mary Cherry whom I saw run in the first Radio Two Dublin City Marathon. She's encouraging. I'm walking more than running now. The rain's cold and pierces my running gear like tiny spears. The headband is certainly unnecessary now. A tall, bearded man is in trouble on my left. We exchange a few words and a handshake. A little girl offers a bar of chocolate which is soft, sticky and as oozy as my brain and it's downhill with a rock band playing on a platform at the left. Someone asked, 'Did you see Charlie?' I didn't.

I wave my arms or what passes for waving and then let them fall again. Some person shouts 'dance Donncha!'. I try. Obviously madness has set in. A girl from Athlone wearing green and a Galway man join me. We are running under a bridge somewhere around the 22-mile mark. Walls, large, small, God-made, man-made and all conquerable are everywhere. Two friends behind me are talking.

'Can we speed it up?'

'You must be joking!'

Then all the pent-up emotions and frustrations of marathon day are unleashed.

'You go on', she says, 'that's what you wanted all day anyway.'

'That's right, that's all the thanks I get, you stupid shagger.'

'Who the hell do you think you're fooling?' she pauses for breath and everyone is laughing – weak bouts of exhausted humour babbling on frothing lips. This is madness and we're into Fairview. The rain has eased and I spare a thought for the unknown lady somewhere in Finglas who gave me the run of her toilet facilities and a quick cup of tea. God bless you missus. The shuffling is instinctive now. A runner stops and drinks a pint of Guinness. His throat is gobbling like a turkey.

The wounded, the weak and the brave feel cheated and angry. A young Garda says, 'ye're all right boys, 'twon't be long now'. The firemen are out in Tara Street clapping rhythmically one two, one two. The mid-marathon silences are over. The kind man in green is encouraging and sustaining me with talks about my long walks. He talks us into Lincoln Place and round the square. We're discussing and enjoying the beauties of Georgian Dublin. I enthuse about life in Dublin in the eighteenth century. 'Didn't they have it good?'

'Were you ever in Bath?' I wasn't, but I know Jane Austen thought well of it.

The slate-grey beauty of Dublin on a rainy day in 1984 enfolds us and tears are close. I see my son Feargal, 'could you stop for a photograph?' he asks. The question is could I start again? And then finally the crowds take over urging, cheering, cajoling, willing, willing us all down the long Golgotha of Leeson Street and into the Green.

I feel like John Treacy, Carlos Lopez, de Castella, Ronnie Delaney, Joe Barry, Director General of RTE, even God himself. It's finished – I'm finished. Noel Carroll is generous in his welcome. Peter Stokes is here again. 'I never doubted you', he said, after a few words with Jimmy Greally. It's twilight and still they are coming in. I pause and clap and clap. I hadn't done that all day. All the runners, all the record breakers all the dreamers of wild and fantastical dreams are winning their Radio Two Dublin City Marathon of 1984 and I too was there.

The Longest Walk of All!
Donncha's Ireland Walk

I decided to devote my summer holidays in 1985 to REHAB and was privileged to walk through every county in Ireland in that wet and miserable month of August. More than IR£100,000 was collected and I was much enthused by the mighty efforts of REHAB through its active management, its unselfish regional committees and Eileen Kerr and Noel Greene, both superb fundraisers and my companions through all the 1,000 mile odyssey. By the end of it, Ireland was done and I was very nearly done for myself!

Buswells Hotel was a breakfast rendezvous and there I met Dick Burke, Tipperary man and TD; Henry Mountcharles, the owner of Slane Castle; Frank Flannery, the chief executive of REHAB; Stephen Farrelly of REHAB, my own family and Pat McInerney and Ann O'Rahilly from RTE. Conversation was desultory. I wondered what walking over 1,000 miles in 30 days and touching every county would be like. I kept my thoughts to myself. Jokes were unavailing. Self-preservation and resolve were paramount.

It began on 1 August, a quiet and dry morning. I had hardly slept at all the night before. We had pre-walk celebrations in Trim hospital, Dunleer and Slane Castle where Paddy Reilly performed.

Slane was our starting point. Cars, trucks, flags, banners and people waited. My son, Donal, as usual was at my elbow, companion of many a walk and many a marathon. He was a reflection of me and I an image of him intermingled in courage and a sense of adventure. I draw, too, from his youth. *Morning Ireland,* by phone, gave me what they now call 'a great buzz.' Of course, I'd complete the course, I said, and then added for myself, 'even without training'. Television news was waiting and I said the usual confident words, smiled the usual smile and hoped for fine weather every day. Donncha, what a hopeless hope!

A lone garda waved us on and I realised for the first time that my first day's growth of beard had begun. I would not shave until my journey was over. Up that first hill I thought of Francis Ledwidge, the poet of Slane, who often walked these same roads and of St Patrick, who lit his paschal fire up there to my left. I'm not the first to walk here! This great walk was led by a piper who manfully blew his way up the long first hill. Henry Mountcharles reminded me of others who had travelled here

'One of the most famous folk to travel this road', he confided, 'was King George IV. He travelled to Slane at least twice. You see he had a wild passion for Lady Conyngham who lived there. It is said that the long straight road from Dublin to Slane was built by him'. I suppose it helped to speed up matters. Did I care?

As we approached Collon I stepped up the pace. This is a first-day ploy and is almost always guaranteed to dull the competitive edge of casual joiners in the walk. We climbed the tough, muscle-tweaking hill and passed by Mellifont Abbey; this was the first Cistercian house in Ireland and home of the great scholar An tAthair Colm Cille O Corbui who always signed himself Manach agus Sagart. He also kindly sent me a Mass card of the late Dan Breen who died on 27 December 1969. It reads 'Let us be brothers thou and I, I and thee, seeing that we are the sons of Him who is my Lord and also thine.' May he rest in peace.

An tAthair Colm Cille signed my copy of 'An Biobla Naofa' as did the late Cardinal Tomás O'Fiaich, Ardeaspag Ard Mhacha, and who sent me a Christmas card following the demise of *Highways and Byways*:

> Brón orm nar éirigh níos fearr leis an iarracht úd ach ar a laghad scríobh mé chuig Stiúrthóir RTE láithreach – Tomás.

A tall young man strolled effortlessly along by my side. He was a REHAB trainee and hardly spoke to me. Then, he surprised me. 'Who are you?' he asked. I looked sideways. He was serious! I said my name. Silence.

'What are you doing here?'

'Walking', I said, 'like yourself'. A big pause.

'So you're the man', he smiled. He wondered where I worked.

'RTE', I said.

'One or Two?' he asked. I explained.

No one talked for a mile or so.

'I never listen to either, they're all news and weather, mostly bad!' he said.

A band played as we came into Dunleer. On the outskirts of the town I was met by Padraig Faulkner, TD and former Minister for Education and his wife and by an enthusiastic local REHAB Committee and several generous ladies from Monasterboice.

Castlebellingham signalled rain that was to follow me like nemesis for every day of the walk. A certain Colonel Thomas Bellingham, who acted as a guide to William of Orange, lived there. In the churchyard is buried Dr Thomas Guither who introduced frogs to Ireland and Napper Tandy, who asked the rhetorical question, 'how is poor old Ireland and how does she stand?' or so the song says, also lies buried here. The first day ended in lashing rain in Dundalk and I had the bridal suite all to myself in the Derryhale Hotel. Diary reads – 'bed 2.00 a.m. Raining'.

Day followed day and gig-filled night followed as sure as bed-time was late-time and shower pursued shower. Splendidly organised, the walk was a massive success. Portadown, where I spoke at several Sunday Masses, presented the first signs of negativity. Walter Love and Radio Ulster told the world that I would be coming their way. Generally, a good idea but not on that Sunday. Everyone was out!

Unknowing, I set off in the pouring rain. Ted Berry from RTE and my son Donal were my silent companions. Suddenly the rain increased and emptied itself all around me. A Hiace van sat by the roadside, its back doors open. I bade them, 'Morning, men'. They just looked. The road seemed suddenly narrow and flinty surfaced. I was uneasy and with every good reason. The road markings proclaimed, 'UVF'. Inside a low wall, not far from the van, three men stood armed. They wore paramilitary style gear and didn't speak.

The 11.00 Sunday morning was chill. Ted suddenly seemed encouraged. 'Comhaltas up ahead', he remarked. Donal said, 'this is the Birches'. As we drew up to the little flute-playing and bodhran-beating group. 'Morning lads', his Longford accent sounded strained. The reply was definite: 'fuck off, you Fenian bastard', which he did.

We were now ten reluctant yards from the young musicians. We were walking closer together. Was it all to end here on a hate-filled, rain-soaked road in Co. Armagh? Anger and a weary sadness enveloped me. A dark-eyed girl said, 'yez are collectin'.

'Yes,' I said.'Would you like to help?' The looks were stony. The answer like before seemed their only form of communication:

'Fuck off, you Fenian bastards.' Threat, danger, fear walked close together.

'Speed up boys', I whispered. 'Don't let them see that we're afraid,' Insult after insult followed us. Some 20 youngsters played 'The Sash' and chanted 'The Queen' while others pounded the back and sides of their van. It was a lonesome and fearful road that reached behind us as a silent and thoughtful trio came to a bridge and our pursuers thankfully turned back and left us. The village of Killyman (evocative name in English-Irish script) – an old couple stood at their door. 'A bad day for harvesting'. I ventured.

His reply said it all, 'Aye, aye, but it is a great day for walkin', walkin' fast.' I knew exactly what he meant!

Further on and around several corners a roadside sign read 'Fuck 1690, we want an action replay'. We just wanted our lunch in Dungannon. 'Ye had quite a morning', the manager said. We ate our sandwiches quietly and happily. It was suddenly great to be alive.

The walk went the way of all walks – on and on. The nineteenth day was crucial, I developed my first and only serious injury – a shin splint on my left leg. The papers carried the heading: 'Donncha limps into Nenagh'. Words like 'struggles, scrambles' or even 'falls' might well describe my state. Osmond Bennett, the masseur motor-man from Johnstown, Co. Kilkenny was called and set about his business in the corner of a pub late-evening in Nenagh. I had no evening meal. I couldn't face it or the encouraging words that would go with it.

It was still dark and wet as I rose reluctantly in Nenagh at 5.30 a.m. The 'shin splint' was quiet although Ossie had warned me to take it easy. A *Cork Examiner* van driver gave me a copy of 'the paper'. 'You're one of our own, boy', he said. It carried news of my 'limp'. Frank Flannery, who would walk with me all day, covered up against the torrential rain and the great gusts of wind that battered the backs of our legs. My rain gear split at the zip. Tough.

A couple drove by in the sickly dawn light, then stopped and returned. The question, often repeated in the coming days was simple, 'how's th'oul leg?' They donated £1. Progress was gingerly, no pain as yet. Trees and hedges were clearer and the day dawned cold and showery. Munster would be like everywhere else. I wondered quietly about survival. I saw Silvermines to my left. Great nights there once upon a time crossed my mind. There would be other great nights up there in Newport with my dear friends Eddie Thornton and Harry Murphy. I didn't know that then, of course. The future is best left to itself! Long nights in Rearcross and presenting my own show, *Where now Caitlin*, on a summer in the past in the lovely village of Puckane, when I, like all the audience, enjoyed the great playing of Paddy O'Brien and his daughter Eileen. It helped to pass a long, wet morning waiting for pain!

I remembered the night when a bald husky American, who came on two nights, said 'lovely show'. I asked the quiet man his name. He answered simply 'Gene Kelly'. You could have knocked me down with a feather. He was a wonderful guest on *Highways and Byways* and I'll always remember his modest kindness. The quiet rainy peace of an August morning on the road to Birdhill accorded well with my memories.

Killaloe brought us to Co. Clare and across the Shannon over the Twelve-Arch bridge where patriots are remembered in stone, and up the hill to the dark, windswept church and the rippling, dancing accordion-playing of Martin Connolly. A lady in a passing car, somewhat misguidedly called me, 'a little saint'. Jim Turnbull who dealt with our money matters brought good news. The day's takings were up to scratch.

Betty Purcell and Jim Jennings from RTE stopped to talk on their way to Lisdoonvarna. They tramped with me for a mile or so. When they had gone, Nell McCafferty and Nuala O'Faolain stopped and were cheerfully encouraging. There was music as we climbed towards the turn-off for Castleconnell, and Martin McCabe, President of Comhaltas offered tea and welcome. It was mid-afternoon in the village of Mick Mackey and the men of Ahane.

At four o'clock a regular pattern developed. My shin-splint woke up and I lapsed into my usual painful silence. Frank Flannery, cheerful companion on a wet day, began to show signs of distress. The morning walkers and talkers became the afternoon hobblers. Conversation was a thing of the past. I began to hate the signposts. Were they not always wrong? Eamon de Stafort, Gaelic Leaguer and indefatigable worker for all things good and Irish in the Shannon region, and Maire offered support and encouragement. Later he told me that when he saw the look on my face, he wasn't sure whether or not to talk! I was speechless with pain and Limerick was still more than an hour away.

On the outskirts of Limerick I was joined by the spry and lively Willie 'Whack' Gleeson, a walker and giver of blood without parallel. He leant towards the odd pithy and thought-provoking phrase like describing my walk as 'child's play' adding, 'Sure I'd walk from Nenagh to Limerick before my breakfast!' He meant no harm and I am sure he would, but before I could do anything I visualised the heading in the paper on the following day: 'Injured Broadcaster Strangles Octogenarian!' I always remember him with affection. Michael Noonan, then Minister for Justice, joined us and led us into Limerick on this my first full day walking with a shin splint. We all talked unknowingly on the local pirate radio station. Imagine, a Minister of Justice, a member of RTE staff and Frank

Flannery, a member of the RTE Authority breaking the law, in rainy unison!

* * *

I should explain much of the off-road activities on the foul August nights. The REHAB organisation was so brilliantly organised that 'Donncha's Ireland Walk' was a viable fundraising activity for most of every 24 hours. The walk itself usually began pre-dawn and often concluded in the dark, averaging some 25 miles per day which meant that the grand total walked was somewhat more than the 1,000 miles anticipated – more, in fact, like 1,300 miles.

'Gigs,' night-time functions were just as strenuous as the walks. Stephen Farrelly usually drove me to the pub and hotel functions, often covering up to 50 or 60 miles per night and encompassing as many as five different 'gigs'. The modus operandi was simple. The entourage would arrive, loudspeakers blaring, at a country pub, pipe band or piper would tune-up, Donncha arrives, marches into the pub, introduced to audience, sings a few songs, as 'Bucket Collection' proceeds, rush Donncha back to the car and then on and on through the night. Donncha and entourage remained in relatively good terms throughout.

To say that the walk was demanding was putting it mildly. I had promised myself to REHAB body and soul during that August. They took me at my word. The hospitality was incredible, not to say relentless. During that walk, Ireland reached out to me and after it I was never the same.

I mentioned in passing earlier that I had a day's growth of beard. This was a promise that I had made to Bill O'Herlihy, who was acting as PRO for REHAB, that I would grow a beard until £100,000 was raised for the charity. I did and it was, some three days from the end.

I made one major miscalculation. I planned to arrive in Croke Park on All-Ireland Sunday with Cork in the hurling final. I was so wrong. On a day of crying rain by the shores of Lough Neagh, I learned that Galway had done it again! It was all poetic justice, well sort of anyway! And it rained every day during that month of August 1985.

The Promised Land

That great REHAB walk had really fired my boilers. I suddenly awakened to new excitements after a few fallow years. I was rediscovering Corkery's hidden Ireland. But where would I turn to next, which door would I need to open, which road should I take? The answers came before Christmas in 1985, when I was visiting my friends Tom and Angela Phelan. During a rare silence, Susan Hamilton, who had close links with Israel, and who had at this stage listened more or less patiently to hurling talk with Angela's father, Tom, said, 'did you ever think of walking the Holy Land? How would you like to walk the Bible? You could be a modern Good Samaritan'. Silence, a small silence. No, I had never thought of walking outside of Ireland. The Holy Land had never crossed my mind. Still, perhaps ... Susan Hamilton is not one for allowing grass grow under her suggestion – or my walking feet!

We met in the Shelbourne Hotel the following morning. The weather was cold and frosty, not like the travel brochures of Israel. They showed the usual brown and shapely bodies, the usual blue and sun-dappled seas with their inevitable mystical and misty mountain background. It was tempting – but walking it? Well, she had contacts in Israel and wasn't the President one of our own? It was all a foregone conclusion. What I needed more than anything else was a close-up look at the Holy Land through the eyes of a Baedeker. I got more than I bargained for!

Karl Baedeker is surely the father of world travellers. The name Baedeker has become synonymous with accurate and useful information delivered, especially in the early editions, in a lovely, if perhaps. idiosyncratic style. The very first edition of the handbook appeared in 1875 and the edition which I managed to get my hands on, thanks to the splendid library of the Irish Dominicans in Tallaght, is the 'Fifth Edition, Remodelled and Augmented' and was published by Baedeker in Leipzig in 1912. Of special interest to me is the fact that: 'In spring the scenery is at its best and the vegetation fresh and vigorous'. There is a small secret note of warning to our Israel travellers. 'A visit to Palestine should not be begun before the middle of March, as many rainy days in that month are still frequent'.

Reading further, I thank the Lord for all the travel arrangements made on our behalf by Alan Benson of Easy Travel. What indomitable travellers they must have been in those days – and how they earned their visit. For our own journey, travellers would be advised to bring the lightest of clothes, the best of running shoes and copious supplies of vaseline! Mr Baedeker is a little different.

> The traveller should take with him a plaid, an overcoat and two suits of clothes ... dress clothes are hardly necessary ... a waterproof coat is essential in the spring .... woollen shirts, undershirts and drawers afford protection against catching cold. The red fez should be avoided, the hat being nowadays the recognised symbol of the dignity of the European.

There is no mention whatever of sun tan lotions, creams or vaselines but health is not forgotten.

> A sun umbrella will be found useful, grey or blue spectacles to shield the eyes from the glare of the sun. Unripe fruit should be avoided. Quinine (three grains daily) against fever; for neuralgia, chlordyne; for headache or rheumatism, phenacetin or aspirin; for the eyes; boracic of zinc lotion; for chaffed sores due to riding, tincture of arnica or Elliman's embrocation; gentle aperients such as cascara sagrada or castor oil should not be forgotten.

Obviously 'hangover' was unheard of, and there was no Osmond Bennett available in those days! But there is one last vital piece of advice:

> Light cases of diarrhoea may generally be cured by rest in a horizontal position and a diet of rice or arrowroot (which should always accompany the traveller) and milk.

Weapons we are told were unnecessary on the main routes but they did have their purposes: 'Weapons add a great deal to the importance to which the "Frank" is regarded by the natives'. Now we come to the part of Mr Baedeker's advice which probably applies as much today as it did a century ago.

Under the heading, 'Intercourse with Orientals', he includes the following gems:

1. Most Orientals regard the European traveller as a madman.
2. A beggar may be silenced with the words 'Allah ya'tik' (May God give thee)
3. No enquiry should be made after the wives of a Moslem!
4. Even looking at women in the street or in a house is considered indecorous.
5. Visitors (to a Moslem home) are always supplied with coffee.
6. To be passed over when coffee is being handed around is deemed an insult.
7. Familiarity should always be avoided.
8. Smuggled tobacco can be had everywhere.
9. The waiter is called in oriental fashion by clapping the hands and calling 'oh boy!'

10. Fridays (baths) are to be avoided.
11. The public baths are always cleanest in the early morning.

With these gems of Baedeker, I felt well qualified to face anything! My mind was in a fever, but, in an hour or so I had formulated a bold plan. Even though I did not know it at the time, it would survive and prosper almost without alteration.

The plan envisaged that each walker would raise a minimum of IR£2,000 for the charity, as well as his or her fare. It was simple, but like many such schemes, it needed plenty of hard work. I drove across Dublin to the Irish Wheelchair Association headquarters in Clontarf and there, over coffee, presented my plan to Phil O'Meachair and Peter Stokes. Philo was, as usual, blunt and succinct. 'Well Donncha, we have never failed with you before. We're with you. Go ahead agus beannacht Dé ar an obair'. I hopefully suggested a target of 50 people for the Irish Wheelchair Association. I then continued my act of faith and hope at REHAB headquarters. Frank Flannery and Stephen Farrelly were equally enthusiastic and before I left, phones were ringing! My last stop was almost on my own doorstep. I dropped into John Duffy, at St Vincent's Hospital. As luck would have it, Margaret Heffernan, the honorary fundraiser for that time was in his office. She had no doubts – St Vincent's was in.

We were up and running. I rang Susan Hamilton, still not sure whether or not I was dreaming. She was not. She suggested Alan Benson of Easy Travel as tour agent, and this was one of the best decisions to emerge from those early deliberations. Now, I'm a great believer in luck, and a least on this occasion, it seemed that fortune had favoured the brave. I was about to pay a pre-Christmas visit to the Irish peace-keeping force with UNIFIL in the Lebanon and, on the way, I had an opportunity to meet with two women in Tel Aviv who would be central to 'Donncha's Holy Land Walk'. These were Zelda Harris and Linda Levine from the BIPAC (Britain/Israel Public Affairs Committee) organisation in Israel. At first, like everyone else, they were somewhat mystified. But when they had finished asking questions and making suggestions, I knew that I still had a lot of work to do.

Back home, Christmas 1985, was an amalgam of pudding and plans, and early in January I set off once again for the Holy Land. Security at London Airport was tight but comforting, and when I landed at Ben Gurion Airport, I met Joe Brett, the man who was to be our guide. We drove to Netanya, which is North of Tel Aviv on the Mediterranean coast, where we had arranged to meet Zelda and Linda later in the morning. Then the four of us sat down, and hammered out the route and the travel arrangements.

The route over which we drove during my first few days in Israel would take us along the path of Jesus, from Nazareth to Cana, to Tiberias, Capernaum and down the Jordan Valley to Jericho, completing our journey in the Holy City of Jerusalem. We laid our final plans sitting by the Sea of Galilee, drinking a good vintage of Carmel Israeli wine, while I sampled St Peter's fish for the first time. (This fish – of which you will hear more later – is known locally as the Musht. It is only caught in the sea of Galilee). Joe and I make out detailed mileages for the walk, which would be of six days' duration.

Throughout the entire walk, we would also be accompanied by an Israeli police escort and an ambulance, in case of accidents or sunstroke. The red-and-cream-coloured buses of the Nazareth Transport and Tourist Co. Ltd. would also become a familiar (and often welcome) sight, as they ferried us to the starting point of the walk each day, collecting us at our ultimate destination, and shadowing us throughout our journey, stopping to supply us with fresh drinking water every half hour en route.

The air-conditioned buses would also be at the disposal of anyone who wanted to rest their weary feet or get out of the strong sunshine. When we would enter the West Bank area, where the Jordan Valley forms the border between Israel and Jordan, we would have an Israeli military escort with us until we reached Jericho.

Back in Dublin, at least once a week thereafter at 8.30 a.m., the three charities, Susan Hamilton, Alan Benson and I met at the REHAB offices. Business was brisk and generally good humoured around that long boardroom table.

Publicity was another essential and it was generously provided. The Press, both national and provincial, rallied round. However, not everyone was so kind. Why is it that those who have power to do so much good can descend to such venial depths? There is no doubt that Terence MacSwiney was right when he said that it is not they who inflict the most but they who endure the most who are the victors. RTE television showed an initial interest, but soon dropped out of the frame! *Donncha's Sunday* and the *RTE Guide* would both do justice – indeed the coverage by the *Guide* was quite magnificent, and a great tribute to the enlightened editor, while journalist Linda Kavanagh and photographer Eve Holmes enriched the walk by word and picture.

Myles MacWeeney reported for the *Irish Independent* on a regular basis, as did Michael Commins for *The Connaught Telegraph*.

There was also a surprise in musical terms. Dermot Kelly, the singing Bank Of Ireland manager in Limerick put pen to paper and with the willing assistance of Denis Allen of 'Limerick, You're a Lady' fame, and well-known pianist Maurice Foley, produced a vibrant song:

DONNCHA IN THE DESERT

(To the air of Slattery's Mounted Fut!)
You've heard of Ronnie Delaney and Eamon Coghlan too,
And how their feet were famous from here to Katmandu,
But there's another pair around made famous by the sand,
Tis' Donncha's SIZE ELEVENS that tramp the Holy Land.
He walked to help the wheelchairs, St. Vincent's and REHAB,
To raise some funds and in between to dissipate the flab,
And all the Arabs shouted as he went marching past:
Here comes the new Messiah, Donncha's here at last.

(Chorus)

And, into the desert went the gallant motley crew
Doctors, Sisters, Nurses and couple of Gardai too
Twenty goats from Dingle and an ass from the County Clare
Hand in hand through sea and sand, just for love and care.

They reached the sea of Galilee so wondrous to behold
The Lord walked on the waters there, or so the story goes
There were no boats nor timber floats to get the crew across
What will we do? It's up to you, Donncha you're the boss.
He put his agile brain to work and suddenly he said :
Line up ten thousand camels and put them tail to head.
They climbed upon their backs that stretched across the stormy sea
And humped it all the across the Sea of Galilee.

Chorus (as before)

They walked for days through sun and haze, the going it was tough!
A bursar from St. Vincent's said 'Boss I've had enough'!
Me feet is sore, me clothes is tore, I think I'll take a rest'.
Till Donncha found him lying down and jumped upon his chest.
'Look here my man, this is no time for sittin' on your ass,
The Lord was here for forty days, so surely you can last
Till we reach Jerusalem, a sight so fair to see,
Any more lip you're off the trip and home by CIE.

Chorus (as before)

Dublin Airport was full of excitement for our first departure. Walkers and friends gathered together. Colm Murray of RTE television news saw us off in two languages. Eve Holmes from the *Guide* 'shot' me tying my shoes! Garda Commissioner Eamonn Doherty who would be joining us later in Tiberias, came to see 22 of his 'boys' on their way, among whom was Matt Connor, Garda and courageous Offaly man who made the long journey in his wheelchair. We all felt bravery and drew quiet consolation from his silent strength. Lucy Johnston, our official photographer 'captured' everyone and the sun actually shone. Someone thought it was an apparition! We flew El Al from London to Tel Aviv, while Aer Lingus did the honours as far as London.

I often wonder since about the man with the overcoat. He wondered in Dublin if it would be fine in Israel. 'I always bring my overcoat wherever I'm going' he said, 'especially to matches, and you know they say 'tis often cold at night in the desert'. The next time I spoke with him was when we were walking from Jericho. He was nearly naked. I wonder if he fell among thieves!

For our third pilgrimage in 1998 we had some 300 pilgrims, a planeload, and El Al brought us all the way, so we sampled their security at home. It was their first ever flight into Dublin, and there were great celebrations. I must say that this made life a lot easier, less tiring and more pleasant for everyone. This year, people were not so easily lost. It saved me a few tasks, like explaining to a rather harassed El Al woman in London that a missing suitcase really did belong to Fr X who had only loaned it for the trip and would be needing it tomorrow to go on holidays himself. And how do you explain that: 'no, there is no direct train service to Grouse Hall but if you ring the Post Office my friend Aine will take the message!' It's very hard to explain things to foreigners, especially at London Airport. They are, as a Kerryman said, 'a biteen slow'. By the way, that suitcase was eventually found. I hope too that Fr X had a pleasant holiday!

Images of Jerusalem

Last night I lay asleeping,
There came a dream so fair,
I stood in old Jerusalem
beside the Temple there,
I heard the children singing
and ever as they sang
Methought the voice of angels
from heaven in answer rang
Methought the voice of angels
from heaven in answer rang.
Jerusalem, Jerusalem, lift up your heart and sing,
Hosanna in the highest, hosanna to your King,
Hosanna in the highest, hosanna to our King.

Our walkers have been twice received at the Presidential Palace in Jerusalem. On the first occasion, we were warmly welcomed by President Chaim Herzog. I shall never forget the emotional moment when I stood up before our great and generous walkers and formally tried to express with some coherence our happiness, excitement and pride at being received by 'one of our own' – the sixth President of the State of Israel. It was cool in the great hall, but as I began to speak – first in Irish, then in English – the 'nerves' forced out a few beads of sweat. It was a great moment to see the 'home-made' Irish tricolour, which our walkers had proudly carried from Bethany to the Holy City, laid side by side with the blue and white Star of David flag of Israel. I managed a few formal phrases, made a little easier by the feeling that I was speaking on behalf of some of the greatest, bravest, and most generous people in the world.

> We have walked all the way from Nazareth to Tiberias, to Capernaum and Bet Shean, through the burning desert, down the long hot road to Jericho, on to Bethany. Now, today, unlike many of the Jews in the Diaspora, we are here – not as they crave 'next year Jerusalem' – but this great day is ours.

I paused for breath and also, if the truth be known, for a little ripple of applause. It never came! For once the Irish seemed transfixed! I pressed grimly on:

we come, representatives of a great and ancient nation, proud to be here, to greet another great and ancient nation and especially to greet you Mr President, one of our own.

Then there was applause, plenty of it. President Herzog replied:

First of all, let me assure you that I understand practically every word of Gaelic you said. I am still full of memories of a very historic visit to Ireland – the first state visit by a President of Israel to Ireland – and I can only say that I am looking forward, sooner or later, to returning the wonderful hospitality to President and Mrs Hillery. We wish to express our kindest appreciation to everyone for the wonderful reception we received in Ireland. Tell Ireland that we look forward to receiving many more groups like yours in Israel. You will always be welcome, and I hope you will always feel at home.

After this the President mingled with and joined in very informal conversation with the group. Another year, the president was abroad during the time of our visit, we were cordially received at his residence by one of his aides, Shulamit Nardi, who accepted, on his behalf, a Galway Crystal vase that we had brought from Ireland. She enthralled our walkers. Her warm and obviously deeply-felt love of her country struck a chord in many hearts, not least my own. Eileen Kerr of REHAB was heard to remark that I nearly stood up and saluted the flags. She was almost right, and why not?

Later on, Shulamit and I sat and talked in the sunshine of the Presidential gardens. When I shivered, she reminded me that there is a considerable difference in temperature between Jerusalem, 2,500 feet above sea level and the Dead Sea which is 1,290 feet below. In the course of one day's walking, we climbed some 4,000 feet. Indeed, when it is sometimes cool in Jerusalem, it can be ferociously hot and stuffy less than 30 miles away. The Presidential gardens contain many fine olive trees, most of them transplanted from other parts of Israel. Shulamit was herself 'transplanted' from America to The Holy Land, in 1934. She knew Hebrew and Yiddish since her New York childhood, for her people had carefully and lovingly cultivated all the old values of the Jewish people. When she reached the Holy Land, it was in no way strange. It was really like coming home. I wondered how one survives in a land which is constantly at war, constantly defending, coping, surviving. How does a nation emerge from a perpetual cycle of warfare, where joy and grief are so inextricably linked? 'You survive with great losses', she said sadly.

Families are perpetually scarred. There is always mourning in Israel. Perpetual mourning, however, leads to very positive dedication. The country is dotted with projects in memory of the dead – some are aesthetic, others are economic – but all are inspiring.

Our conversation then turned to the Kibbutz movement, which, she suggested, sets standards for others and helps people to 'become more devoted to the general weal'. No matter how difficult life is, there is always an edge of laughter in Israel'. She has a nice Jewish sense of humour. 'You know, at least three celebrations of Christmas take place in Israel', she remarked. 'It goes on for a long time. The only time Christian leaders seem to meet here is when they meet once a year at Christmas time in the Presidential Palace. They are probably too busy otherwise!'

She would like Israel to be 'more egalitarian'. Peace, she hoped, would come sooner and more evenly. She had hoped for more co-operation between Arab and Jew. There were, of course, successes.

> Relations with Egypt are good, more credit to that great man, the late President Anwar Sadat. He paid the full price and he knew that he would. Peace comes closer, inch by inch, gesture by gesture. It is better to talk about discussions than to have no talk at all. King Hussein of Jordan may like to talk in the future. The Moroccans seemed poised for some form of detente. There is always hope. If there is not that, there is nothing.

We walked towards the gate, there was time for one more question, one more answer: 'yes, Moses is my favourite character in the bible', she told me. 'He had so many blessings and so many sorrows. The people he was leading gave him so many problems'. She paused, looked at me, and smiled. 'More than yours did, I expect. I sympathise with him. He never reached the Promised Land. He was so great – the man who heard the Divine Word, transmitted it to others and shaped a special people'.

As I left the presidential gardens, all the glorious scents of an Israeli spring wafted across the flower beds. The champagne air of Jerusalem engulfed the senses. It was a day to be lyrical, a day for poetry, a day to remember the great man Moses in verse.

> The rich man in his castle,
>
> The poor man at his gate,
>
> God made them, high or lowly,
>
> And ordered their estate.
>
> By Nebo's lonely mountain,
>
> On this side of Jordan's wave,
>
> In a vale in the land of Moab,
>
> There lies a lonely grave.

This little poem, 'The Burial Of Moses' was written by Cecil Frances Alexander in 1854. She also wrote 'All Things Bright And Beautiful' and 'Once In Royal David's City'. Incidentally, when Donncha's Inis

Eoghain Walk took place some years ago I never knew that Ms Alexander had a connection with the peninsula. It's a long strange road from Fahan to Mount Nebo! HV Morton, whose evocative and splendidly written *In The Footsteps Of The Master* has hardly ever left my bedside, has described with accuracy and style the difficulties of 'capturing' the Holy City.

> One is shown all kinds of sights in Jerusalem which maybe are open to doubt – such as the very spot on which the cock crowed when St Peter denied his Lord – but one looks at them with respect for the piety which created them, and with distaste for the principle which profits from them. On the Mount of Olives, however, one knows that these little stony tracks are the very paths that He must have taken and that they are marked more truly with the imprint of His feet than on any rock within the golden shrine.

Indeed, the more I visit the Holy Land and the more I read about it, the more I am struck by certain anomalies. How can you take seriously the solemn notices ordering 'modest dress' in holy places when, as you look, an importuning trader offers you 'an authentic plastic crown of thorns' (special price $2) – all within yards of Calvary! God and Mammon are often inextricably intertwined in Jerusalem.

One of the most unusual examples of giving is to be found at the lower end of Keren Hayesod Street, which leads into beautiful gardens not too far from the King David Hotel and near the archaeological diggings at Herod's family tomb. Here you will see a windmill, standing alone and strange. This is the Montefiori Windmill, bequeathed to the poor Jews of Jerusalem by Sir Joseph Montefiori. An article in a London newspaper describes the construction process of the 'Yemin Moshe Windmill', which was completed in 1857. Under the heading 'Windmill at Jerusalem' it reads 'Sir Joseph Montefiori has caused to be erected at the foot of Mount Sion, about a quarter mile from the Jaffa Gate, a windmill for the use of the poorer inhabitants of Jerusalem, who had previously the laborious task of grinding their corn by hand mills.' Rather sadly, the mill was never used! The poor Jews, for whom it was intended, were afraid to leave the shelter of their ghettoes and enter into – as they saw it – marauder territory. Baedeker was, as usual, succinct. He knew, even if we did not, exactly where we were. 'The new quarter was given the name of Mishkenot Shaanaim (Dwellings of Peace)'.

The new neat blocks, with their flower gardens and arbours flowing with fragrant creeper, were rebuilt after 1967 and are now homes for artists, writers and musicians. We set off downhill across the valley, and began the short steep climb to the Church of the Dormition and the Cenacle.

The Cenacle, scene of the Last Supper, the upper room where Christ first changed bread and wine into his body and blood, is relatively easily approached. And whether or not we needed a guide, there was one there who never stopped talking even in that bare and peaceful upper room, where all I craved was silence. I suppose he felt that he had to earn his 10 shekels. Over on the Mount Of Olives as the Passover approached, Jesus sent Peter and John into the City of David to find a room for His Last Supper. He was quite specific, 'go and make preparations for us to eat the Passover ... as you go into the city you will meet a man carrying a pitcher of water. Follow him into the house he enters and tell the owner of the house. "The Master has this to say to you: where is the dining-room in which I can eat the Passover with my disciples?" The man will show you a large upper room furnished with couches. Make the preparations there. They set off and found everything he had told them and prepared the Passover.' (Luke 22.7–13).

It was from here that the infant Christian Church grew and developed after the death of Jesus; it was here the Holy Ghost descended and it was here too, that Thomas believed because he had seen and where the risen Jesus gave hope to all who followed: 'Happy are those who have not seen and yet believe'.

All of this seemed far from the guide's mind as he chivvied us downstairs, perfunctorily pointing out that 'it was in that corner he washed their feet'. Never was the miraculous tenderness of Jesus, nor his gentle humanity so absent! We were far away from John: 'I tell you most solemnly, no servant is greater than his master, no messenger is greater than the man who sent him' (John 13:12). The Cenacle is often seen through the eyes of Leonardo da Vinci. His famous fresco has visualised that most famous of suppers. The visitors must visualise while they are there, let neither guide nor friends disturb their concentration in this room. HV Morton's tender evocation brings it all back.

> The hush of a moonlit night wrapped itself about the house of the Last Supper. As the full moon arose, the light would have slanted into it under the awning. There would have been a lamp burning ... and beyond the stillness of the upper room the pinnacles and towers of Jerusalem would be seen lying against the stars ... and Jesus said, 'take, eat: this is my body ... and this is my blood of the New Testament which is shed for many'.

Taken at face value – and with the hindrance of a guide – the upper room was a disappointment! But pause for a moment in the doorway, having climbed the stairs. Look into the room – the bare featureless room – and let time flow over you and, before you know it, the events of that first Mass will almost become real. Incidentally, what is known as the Tomb of David adjoins the downstairs room in the Cenacle. This whole area is now used as a synagogue. The alleged Tomb of David is covered with magnificently embroidered tapestries and laid on it are silver crowns and Torah rolls (the five books of Moses, containing Jewish law). Pilgrims constantly pray here, especially on the Jewish feast of Shavuot which commemorates Moses receiving the ten commandments. It was mid-afternoon when we crossed the alley leading to the neo-Romanesque Catholic Church of the Dormition of our Blessed Lady. This very striking church was built in 1908 and is in the care of German Benedictine monks. The massive towers, visible from many parts of Jerusalem, give the church a fortress-like appearance.

The upper church is decorated with mosaics and bronzes but, for me, the real beauty and atmosphere were to be found in the crypt where, according to Fr Hoade, the Franciscan author and lover of Israel, 'you must admire its concentric compass with the altar of the Dormition in the centre, before which lies in the peaceful slumber of death the statue of the Virgin'. During my visit to the church, a German choir gave a tuneful rendition of 'Salve Regina'. Other pilgrims sat quietly in the coffee shop. Monks did a thriving business in the shop selling holy books and holy things. It seems that Mammon is never far from God.

The sheer weight of history puts Jerusalem almost beyond human comprehension. Christianity, Judaism and Islam are all at home here. David, Mohammed and Jesus all belong here. This beautiful and battle-riven city is the hub of a complicated and disunited world of spirituality. My exploration of that city began many years ago, on the long flight from London to Israel, when an elderly Jewish woman from Manchester enthused about 'our country'. She actually made me envious of her Jewish sense of identity. Now I was in that amazing city, spending the final day of our walk, exploring its beauty and diversity.

We entered the Old City by the Jaffa Gate, and before long were swallowed up in the timeless atmosphere of David Street. Buying, selling, huckstering, bargaining, winning and losing are vividly and electrifyingly central to life here. In this place, the tourist is the raw amateur in the ruthlessly professional, even good-humoured world of shrewd shopkeepers. 'You like some t-shirts ... excellent quality ... suit your size ... 12 shekels for two'. Then, if there is no response 'look here sir, lady ... 10 shekels for two ... I break my heart ... my hungry children.' Ah, of course you are Irish ... we love the Irish more than anyone else ...You from Killarney'. All the time he is assiduously wooing you into his shop. He waxes confidential, 'my friend, my Irish loving friend, you love your

Arab brother ... You are my first customer today ... You know this is really special ... Special for you Irish!'

You mumble that your wife carries the purse. She is moving on. He loses interest in you and protests loudly to her that his children may starve any day now. And, all along this steep and narrow street, business is transacted as it might have been in the time of Jesus. We turn left into the Muristan and the sun is blinding after the scented twilight world of the bazaars. A moustachioed man, looking not unlike Groucho Marx, materialised. His message was cheerful and positive: 'Ah my friends, welcome to my new shop. You are blessed'. I looked around. There was no one else nearby. 'You are very blessed. You are my very first customers today'. First twice in one day. It was almost too much for me! I tried to pass by. He was in agony. 'Ah my friends, by your accent you are Irish'. He had tears in his eyes 'I would love to go there some day ... perhaps you would like to see inside. Perhaps you like tea? Coffee? Lemonade? There is no obligation. Please bless my little shop. Maybe you like to meet Christ first ... I will wait.' It was all a little confusing. He was pointing towards the Basilica of the Holy Sepulchre and uttering the immortal words: 'Christ was crucified in that Church. Mary, his mother, she stab herself to death as he died'. It was too much, more than enough for one day! We began a walk around the outside of the Old City walls in the afternoon. A man offered us hot tea. It was all very Arab, very local. I felt uncomfortably tourist. The spicy smells from the shops, the furious and prolonged horn-blowing, the cries of Arab vendors, the women hurrying by – dark eyed and all wearing yashmaks – contrasted sharply with four very young Israeli soldiers on a street corner. We begin to climb a gentle slope under the wall, where great hunks of rock have sat immutable through the centuries, a constant stony reminder to resident and visitor alike of century after century of troubled history.

The Rockefeller Museum rises up across the road on our left. Like everywhere else, it is white and glaring in the heat. Giant cacti proliferate along the base of its wall. The plants are covered in a film of white dust, smothered in the dry grime of time, making us thirsty for some odd reason. We slake our thirst, the water lukewarm but effective. The museum, which is northeast of Herod's Gate, is named after John D. Rockefeller who endowed it with a bequest of $2 million in 1927 which was a great sum of money at the time. It is situated on historic ground – the very square on which Godefrey de Bouillon and his Crusaders attacked the city on July 15, 1099. On our side of the road, there were welcoming seats under the shadow of the walls. People were resting here in the languid way that is so distinctively middle Eastern. We appeared to be the only ones walking in the shimmering heat. Taxi after taxi went busily by – all full, and all Mercedes. My feet had begun to burn (footsore knowledge is the only way to really know Jerusalem).

Looking back towards the Rockefeller Museum, the cacti in the distance looked like old and shrivelled guardians of what is preserved within. The great spires of the Russian Orthodox Church at the top of the Mount of Olives towered into view. This is, in fact, one of the first sights of Jerusalem for the walkers, encouraging perseverance for flagging spirits and aching feet. Its bulkiness dominates the distant skyline to my left. There, too, in the distance is the skyscraper building of the Intercontinental Hotel. How did they ever get planning permission?

We passed by St Stephen's Gate, now quite inaccurately called the Lion's Gate. This was a scene of strife during the Six Day War in 1967, when Israeli paratroopers stormed it. We passed by the inevitable monument. We reached the Golden Gate. It is sealed. It faces down to where a sign in English, Hebrew and Arabic reads 'Gethsemane'. The Golden Gate was erected in the seventh century. The Arabs call it Bab er Rameh (Gate of Salvation), for this is where both Jews and Arabs believe will be the area of the Last Judgement. The Jews hoped that the Messiah would enter through this gate, so the Arabs, for this reason and for others, sealed up the entrances and buried their dead in front of it.

Finally, having negotiated the road in between, we entered the Garden of Gethsemane, passing by the tomb of the Virgin. We were now on the lower slopes of the Mount of Olives and beginning to climb. At the entrance to the Garden, an Arab stood by a lethargic camel which leered at us with a mouthful of yellow teeth as its owner invited us to be photographed beside it. The word 'camel' is scrawled with impious vulgarity on the wall. A notice tells, 'here Jesus began his passion, suffered and sweated blood'.

In the Garden of Gethsemane that afternoon a group of French tourists broke the silence, for this place, just beyond the city traffic is nevertheless incredibly still. It seems a garden of peace, best savoured without words. The guide shrilled out the Bible story. Cameras attempted to encapsulate a speck of time in this timeless place, where once the history of humankind was changed forever. The old and gnarled olive trees were curiously cool. Some say that a few of these trees are more than 3,000 years old. Some trees are stooped, others are upright. All are ancient, their leaves glistening, whitish in the sun. The Garden is protected from souvenir hunters by a railing. We made our way through the Garden to the Basilica of the Agony of Christ, also known as the Church of All Nations.

In the central apse of this church is the isolated block of rock which projects 25 centimetres above the floor into the central nave. This is the traditional place where the agony of Jesus took place. This holy place is commemorating the great episode in the life of Jesus. The name of the place is 'Oil Press'. The locality was a garden of olives. It was probably furnished with an oil press. The name of Gethsemane has never been changed; this place is at the foot of the Mount of Olives beyond the Kidron Valley. Jesus and his apostles often frequented the place ... three shrines were built here. The first church – Byzantine – of the fourth century, was built here within the time of Theodosius in the second half of the fourth century; the second church – medieval Crusader – was built in the twelfth century and the new church was built in 1920 when the architect was the Italian Antonio Barluzzi.

Having abstracted this information, we entered the church itself; it was dark and silent. Even guides were silent here. There was an atmosphere of evening, a subtle glow of dusk reflected through the windows. Beams of purple, blue and white light are flashed across the aisle, highlighting pillars and reaching up into the high ceiling of the magnificent dome. The chairs, surprisingly enough, are of the ordinary kitchen variety. The great rock dominates all the floor area in the sanctuary. It was cool with no hint of the terrific heat beyond the door. The effect of dusk brought with it a unique meditative atmosphere. The Barluzzi elegance of design, far from diminishing, enriched the mood of Gethsemane. A priest in red, his assistants in white, the tender glow of the altar lamp – all combined in the mystery of this holy place.

Outside the Gate of Gethsemane we turned right, climbing up very steep stone steps. We were heading for the Mary Magdalen Russian Orthodox Church. A child collected a shekel from each of us as we entered the grounds. We came across a wayside shrine set in the wall. It depicted Christ in the Garden of Gethsemane. A little red bulb glowed ineffectually against the afternoon sun, while a legend read, 'watch ye and pray, lest ye enter into temptation' (Mark 14:38). By now one felt well boiled and disagreeably envious of the few nuns and priests who sat having afternoon tea in the delicious shade of their monastery garden. No one asked if I had a mouth on me! The sign firmly said 'Private'.

Another short climb and there was the church, shining white in the sun, its spires reminding me of enormous onions. It was surrounded by the inevitable olive trees. The church itself bore the unmistakeable stamp of Russia in its shape and design. We flopped down on a step and rested for a moment in the shade. The Kidron Valley faced us, its olive trees drawn up like green and dusty soldiers in serried ranks along the hillside.

It struck me that this will be a very crowded place on the Last Day. I wonder where will the Irish fit in? What with the Jews and Arabs buried so near the expected throne of the Divine Judge, I wonder will we get any look-in at all.

Once inside the church we were offered a guide sheet in many languages. The woman in charge apologised. There was none in Irish! The souvenir shop was closed and there was – to be truthful about it – a feeling of musty desiccation. The church was grand in a faded sort of way, with many representations of various events in the life of Mary Magdalen, but it bears no comparison with the Church of All Nations. The Magdalen Church gives one a sad feeling of disuse. Before we left the porch, I read this quite startling notice: 'No admittance to ladies wearing trousers'. The climb was steeper now as we ascended the Mount of Olives. At one point, the actual rock of the Mount of Olives protruded through the roadway and we felt very close to all the pilgrims who ever walked here. It reminded me of another search, another time, when on a boiling Sunday in August, I had toiled up hill after hill in the Holy City of Rome in search of the burial place of the great O'Neill. That journey had proved in vain, but there was no disappointment here.

Through the afternoon silence, I heard the insistent song of tree crickets. Their woody serenade broke through the stillness like a tune of demented timpanists hammering out a burning beat when all other music had ceased. Their unending, unchanging cacophony filtered through the peace of the Mount of Olives, until it seemed that the glare of the sun and the rhythm of the crickets were the only reality. Then the unique dome of the Dominus Flevit Church (the Lord wept) rose gently before us, a reminder that it was somewhere here that Jesus wept over that beloved city. From a distance it looked like a mosque with a cross atop its dome. Even the brightness of the day could not counter melancholy thoughts, echoes of Jesus on his last walk through this place, walking inexorably to his death. Here, all around us, were graves, here from time uncharted. We walked on the silent world of the dead. We paused and watched the Orthodox Hasidic Jews, wearing the traditional side ringlets, as they mourned their dead. There they stood wearing black suits and hats, even in the heat.

We entered the grounds of Dominus Flevit, where just ahead of us, a young man in shorts was quickly supplied with trousers about eight times too big for him, to cover his bareness in this holy place. The elderly Arab gate-keeper kindly offered icy cold refreshing water. We talked in our own tongues, understanding nothing but comprehending everything. Kindness does not come in Arabic or in English, it comes from the heart.

A Mass was being celebrated in German inside the little church. We were the only congregation. The priest continually mopped his brow as his prayers poured through the great window of Barluzzi, and it seemed to us that all of the Holy City seemed covered in prayer. This beautiful church was built in 1955 and Mass is said before the most breathtaking view across the world. Bells rang out across the valley, their echoes vibrating up as far as our eyrie on the Mount of Olives. Outside, the green of the palms counterpointed the glowing world of white sepulchres all around us. Inside the church, even with sunshine streaming in, the small glow of wax candles seemed undimmed. A plaque on the wall read: 'Jesus beheld the city and wept over it' (Luke) this was followed by a tender hopeful verse: 'Here rings anew the love of God's lament; Mankind made for himself, So far from him has strayed; Here, now, the Saviour calleth thee in love; God calleth, calleth, calleth; Repent and come back home'.

A tiny breeze whipped through the palms. A young Franciscan friar held his beads with lip-moving fervour. Suddenly the mood was broken. We were joined by a group of American pilgrims and their hyper, nasal guide. His voice cut through the peace like a corncrake on a harvest twilight. 'See now, gather around, this church is, as you can see, shaped like a tear,' he intoned. 'You got that?', no need to write that down, Mary Jo. I'll give you a cassette for just a few dollars later. Now as I say, this tear-shaped church has little corner spires also shaped like tears. These are stones, corners, if you will, shaped like tear vials. The ancients all kept their tears in vials. Now, when Mary Magdalen washed the feet of the Lord, she did not cry. She just emptied her vials all over him.' We stood up. It was time to go. Vials indeed!

All too soon, we returned to the brutal climb. We passed the tombs of the Prophets and drew our first breath of the afternoon in the Intercontinental Hotel, where we paused briefly for refreshments. The hotel was cool and elegant. I felt sweaty and a bit of a shambles, still no one seemed too put out! There was an Arab wedding reception taking place in the hotel when we arrived. The bride and her bridesmaids were being photographed in the hotel foyer. Finally, the photographer was ready, and the lovely bride posed, wearing on her face that frozen look that gazes down from every wedding photograph the world over. The bridegroom was a fusser! He lurked, leered instead of smiled and was not – if looks were anything to go by – having a great day! Two elderly Arab men, the respective and very respectable fathers, sat behind a table. They welcomed the guests with much smiling and handshaking. As we passed by to the bar, they looked us up and down in a not-unfriendly way, concluding that we did not belong to either side. We sat down, quite exhausted, and were soon demolishing large helpings of ice-cream cake, washed down with delightful mango juice. Getting back on our feet was an effort, but onward we marched up the hill again, past the few mandatory scruffy camels and on towards the village of Et-Tur. It was now five o'clock and we had been climbing for longer than was good for us. We were looking for the Ascension Chapel. My sweater bearing the inaccurate tidings 'Donncha's Israeli Walkers – 1985' was drawing us no little attention. It was about as important to me at that stage as a lighthouse in the middle of the Bog of Allen!

The Chapel of the Ascension stands within the precincts of a mosque. The Arab 'guardians' were friendly, and one shekel saw us into the tiny chapel. I wondered if this was the place of which Luke the Evangelist wrote: 'he led them out as far as towards Bethany, lifting up his hands, he blessed them. He parted from them and was carried up into heaven,' (Mark 24:50-2). Incidentally, followers of Islam also believe that Jesus ascended into heaven. My visit was brief, but the sight of the candle burning on the rock from which is said Jesus ascended more than compensated for a fast-enveloping exhaustion. We set out on the road to Bethphage and marvelled at the great view spreading out across the valleys. It was probably from this village that Jesus, mounted on a donkey, set out for his exciting entrance into a Jerusalem of waving palms and people shouting Hosannas. However, we never reached Bethphage. It seemed to me that local youngsters whom we met on a narrow patch of road were vaguely, if cheerfully hostile. We turned back, uncomfortable and nervous. We were probably wrong. On our way back down the Mount of Olives, we paid a brief visit to the Church of Pater Noster, which commemorates Jesus teaching his apostles the Lord's Prayer, which is written here in 80 languages on slabs of coloured tiles. I hoped to see the Irish version. However, a very irate French nun descended on me and, in a loud voice, announced, 'You must go now, you must go now. It is after hours. We are closing immediately'. There seemed no point in explaining that I was a 'traveller' and an Irish one at that.

So, we made our way as best we could down the dusky slopes of the Mount of Olives, and managed to get taxis back to our hotel. Within minutes, I had fallen into a sleep of utter exhaustion, after what had been a strenuous but rewarding day of exploring the Holy City. Many walkers have kindly sent me highlights from their own diaries and memories.

> Nothing could ever match the emotion I felt when I lifted my eyes from the roadway and heard from all sides 'look, look' ... I saw below me the Holy City spread out in glorious evening sunlight. I sensed euphoria.

Another walker remembers former Chief Rabbi Cohen's warm welcome and the glorious moment when she went solo saying, 'I couldn't refrain from bursting into the same Psalm (121) as sung in the daily prayer of the church today:

> Joy was in my heart alleluia
>
> When I heard them say let us go to God's house
>
> And now our feet are standing alleluia
>
> In your gateways Jerusalem.
>
> Pray for peace in Jerusalem Prosperity to your houses!
>
> Peace inside your city walls Prosperity to your palaces
>
> Since all are my brothers and friends I say peace be with you!
>
> Since Yahweh our God lives here I pray for your happiness.

Since the number of 'pilgrims' familiar with this prayer was limited, it was soon out-sung by a lusty and spirited rendering of 'The Holy City'. Well, the sentiments were the same and I wholeheartedly participated in the moment. Another friend has titled her memory 'Incident in Jerusalem'. There was the one who shall be nameless honoured among the guests at a reception given by David Birkahn. Having taken a bite from a dainty morsel, she looked at the remains of the savoury to behold, winking up at her, her precious front tooth. Disaster! Conversation became somewhat inhibited! The sequel was even more strange! A concerned fellow traveller (a dangerous species) took to the streets of the Holy City in search of super-glue – from Hebrew-speaking merchants. Eventually and after much honest endeavour and highly sophisticated sign language, the glue was obtained. Sad to relate, the repair job was somewhat less than professional. Could the man himself have helped? Now questions must be asked – with perhaps an answer to be given next year. Who was 'the man himself – God? Was it David Birkahn (who is a very prominent and successful dentist in Jerusalem)? Was it Donncha, who was once known to mend a molar or two? Only time will tell! Another walker asked: 'Can anyone imagine 200 Jews or Arabs marching down through Belmullet or Ballyhea?

I'm also reminded myself of that shopkeeper who invited me into his shop near the Church of the Holy Sepulchre. Well – I might as well confess – I succumbed. I went in, drank mint tea, sipped arak, an Arab version of poitín! and listened to soft talk. 'You are a lovely man sir, I like your good taste. There is no obligation, no obligation at all sir. You are my Irish friend, a good man. You sit down and rest and the great God (are you a Catholic sir?) the great God of the Pope will bless you. Now I have an item of furniture which could be either a relic from Byzantium, the top of an ornate table, an expensive wall hanging, a bodhran, or a tray. It faces me every day at home. It belongs to that rare species which comes uniquely at a 'special price for you Irish!' Shalom, Groucho Marx – I look forward to meeting you again next year! I have a few very special memories of my own. Everyone in the Holy Land advised me to meet Larry Elyan, and meet him I did in David Birkahn's home in Jerusalem. He is as lively as a cricket and as outspoken as any true Corkman can be. 'I was born in Cork, in a place called Jewtown', he explained, 'in a block of about 90 houses, there were some half dozen Jewish families, hence the name Jewtown. And although there are very few Jews still living in Cork, that place is still known as Jewtown.

> We were very happy with our neighbours. On one side we had Protestants and on the other, Catholics, all great friends of ours. Mind you, it was a poverty stricken childhood, but everyone seemed happy with their lot.

He came to Israel on his retirement, and never ceased to be surprised at seeing Jews doing everything everywhere. He visited Israel first in 1950 out of curiosity. 'I didn't know what to expect, used to being a minority in Ireland, it amazed me to see Jews everywhere'. Larry had worked in London during his early years and became an actor almost by mistake. He was a member of The Irish Literary Society which met there for lectures and so on, once a month. One of the members was an actress named Una O'Connor. She tried him for a part in a play and he was so successful that he got a second part in another play. Although he was working with the British Civil Service, he was in close touch with happenings at home in Ireland. 'On the establishment of what was called "The Irish Free State", I opted to go home and Una gave me a letter of recommendation to Lennox Robinson,' Larry explained, 'I then met this other very lanky Corkman, with the slightest trace of a Cork accent, who put me on a list of people available for taking part in crowd scenes'. And that was how Larry Elyan became associated with our national theatre. 'The Abbey Theatre in those days had only enough money to pay for four permanent actors', Larry added:

> There was nobody ever like Sara Allgood – I remember her and Eileen Crowe. Yeats was the Director of course. He never saw anyone. You know the story about his appointment with AE (George Russell)? They never met, because one was looking up and the other was looking down! Yeats always looked over everyone's heads. I was picked by Yeats for a part in one of his earliest verse plays, which was being repeated in the Abbey sometime in the late twenties.

Larry well remembers the Yeats' presence. 'You just stood in awe of him'. He saw little of Lady Gregory, who came to Dublin 'only once in a blue moon. They always called her The Old Lady. As a matter of fact,

Denis Johnston's play called *The Old Lady Says No* , which he said is all about Caitlín Ní hUallacháin, is not right. This is all a cod. The point was that he presented this play to the Abbey Theatre first and the reply he got back was, *The Old Lady Says No*. So that's what he called the play!' There were no dissenting voices that evening in the Birkahn garden in Jerusalem.

Larry remembered well Yeats' famous outburst.

> 'You have disgraced yourselves again. This is apotheosis'. I'll never forget when he mounted the platform as they (the audience) were climbing up on the stage at *The Plough And The Stars*. I was there. I was a member of the audience. There was complete turmoil. I remember the stately figure mounting the stage.

Although we were anxious to hear further anecdotes from Larry, at that precise moment, we were called for tea. And we never got a chance to resume that conversation! – maybe some day in heaven.

My thoughts also go back to a darkening twilight when the Holy Sepulchre was almost empty, only a whisper of prayers, foreign yet familiar, disturbed the peace. We were an incongruous group, but more reverent than the Christian guides who touted shekels. Still, this Calvary, this dim gloom is rooted in the heart of the Bible Story. It was here that Jesus suffered indescribably, here he died, from here he rose again. There is no despair here, only hope and belief. The best of humankind is rooted here. If you sit and close your eyes, faith, imagination and Jerusalem will do the rest. This land of the Gospels is rooted in the heart.

It does not matter that Latin, Greek and Copt are in silly confrontation here; their role is peripheral. We, especially those of us who have walked for all those days in the footsteps of the Nazarene, have at last found rest. The walk ended here. HV Morton, who first came to the Holy Land some 50 years ago, wrote movingly and convincingly of the Holy Sepulchre and of us pilgrims.

> In all of them you discover, as they approach the sepulchre, the same strange expression of overpowering emotion. Each seems to think that, having worshipped before the tomb of Christ, he may return to die in peace in his distant home, the wish of his life fulfilled. He has reached the acme of his earthly desire.

It was dark when we left the Holy Sepulchre. The little alleyways were almost still. The traders in David Street had all gone home. The Jaffa Gate was huge and dark against the skies. The moon shone down on the great city. We walked by the home of Theodor Herzl, the man who first dared to dream of a Zionist state. Here the birds of the sun had tucked their heads into folded wings. This was the end of a day, any day in the Holy City.

DONNCHA

For me it was the end of a journey, the end of ten happy days, for tomorrow, we would make the return journey to Dublin. And yet, there is never an ending here. The Holy Land is always with you. Shalom Israel. Go mbeirimid beo ag an am seo arís!

In The Steps Of O'Sullivan Beara

'Donncha's Winter March', a ferocious and savage journey from Glengarriff to Leitrim Village, was undertaken on New Year's Eve 1986 and ended 15 days later in the snow and ice of our destination.

We were following in the footsteps of 1,000 people who marched with Donal Cam O'Suilleabhain Beara on the most fearsome march, or retreat in our history. One thousand people set out and only 35 reached the fort of O'Ruairc of Breifne. They began on New Year's Eve 1602 and struggled into their safe haven 15 days later. His little army marched to survive. My daughter, Sinéad and myself marched for charity. Our cause was that of children, those who each year were brought on pilgrimage to Lourdes for what is known as the Irish National Handicapped Children's Pilgrimage Trust.

The morning of 31 December 1986, 384 years after O'Suilleabhain's departure, dawned and grew misty as we travelled to the little oak glade, Doirín na Fola, above Glengarriff. We were surrounded by O'Sullivans. Bernie O'Sullivan bade us farewell on behalf of the clan in Irish and in English, reciting Canon Dineen's famous poem describing O'Sullivan's feelings as he marched away from his home.

He calls on the bright sun not to sink until he has seen once again the mountains and valleys of his patrimony:

> Go leathad mo shúil ar na sleibhtibh seo ailne
>
> Mar is mór é mo dhúil iad d'fheiscint uair eile

And, then with a few silent handshakes, we slipped and slithered down the hillside on our way to Leitrim.

Glengarriff was still and sleeping as we crept through on our first long climb. Joe Earley, who was *chef d'equipe* on the march, was solicitous.'You look sweaty', he accurately observed. I had planned for a snowy start but the West Cork Riviera was balmy and by the time I got to

Derrycreha National School I was lathered in sweat and struggled out of my 'thermals' when I talked to Gay Byrne on the radio.

Kealkill Post Office was where Barry Murphy and his wife had me feasting on Christmas cake and Irish whiskey before the long trek towards the dark forbidding pass of Keimaneigh. Here the balmy morning gave way to torrential rain and a warm welcome from the Harringtons in the post office. I scribble in my diary that a man at Carraiganass Castle showed me a skull with grass growing from it and informed me that it was the skull of a round head. He carried it in a Dunnes Stores bag!

Night had fallen as we climbed to the sopping windy heights of Gort a'Phlodaigh. Dozens of the locals had joined us. Laughter and the music of tin whistles punctured the hilly darkness. Tales, some tall, some funny and many ghostly were exchanged. We looked across the rainy valley at the windows glowing with Christmas candles. One felt that time past and time present were wedded on our winter march.

We dropped down slowly. Backs of legs ached, the sound of bagpipes stole eerily up the hillside. Through the gloom came Donal Cronin in full piper's regalia. The rain began again, as Donal welcomed us to his land. The O'Sullivans had spent their first night at the Teampaillin at Eachros now Ballingeary, an event so eloquently described by Aodh de Blacam, 'it is likely that no campfires were lit, lest spies from the heights around should detect the lodging place of the fugitive 1,000. Twenty-six miles the column had marched on one terrible day'. As indeed did we!

Oliver O'Brien recorded Donal as he played O'Sullivan's march. There was a memorable party in Cronins. Mrs Cronin had just given birth to a new baby, and I sat by the fire holding the baby, Donal, in my arms while all celebrated his arrival. My daughter Sinéad sat on the other side of the hearth. She, too, would walk the whole journey with me. The baby snuggled contently against me. He would never remember, but this peaceful moment would remain with Sinéad and myself forever. It was so much in strange counterpoint to the death of an O'Sullivan baby on that march all those years before. The field where folklore says the child died was called 'Pairc a Leinbh'.

New Year's Day 1987 found us marching over Maoileann mountain remembering that O'Sullivan had lost his great mare, An Chearc, so called because of her liveliness, in a boghole hereabout. The place was named 'Poll na Circe'. Donal MacSuibhne led us on to Baile Mhuirne and towards the shrine of St Gobnait. Here lay Sean O'Riada, his wife Ruth and among many other, the poet Sean O'Riordáin.

Seán O Sé joined us and remembering his great regard for O'Riada sang 'Mo Ghile Mear' the poem by Seán Clárach Mac Domhnaill. The large gathering joined in the chorus. Seán told us that his uncle Murt O Sé had cycled this same journey on his retirement, had kept a diary, but it was since lost. Sean reminded us that this was history in the making, that here in the company of the dead we were joined to all who went before us.

We made a brief stop at the Mills in Ballyvourney for lunch and headed for the steep climb up the side of Mullachanish heading north: Helen Ní hAodha from Radio na Gaeltachta interviewed me.

Leaving the crowd behind, we trudged past the RTE transmitter, towards the dark woods now flecked with lightly falling snow. The cold bit hard. Through the snow the surrounding mountains rose ghostly and shadowy. Hail shafted down. A woman emerged from a clearing where she was awaiting us. It was Máire Ní Cheallacháin, great woman of camogie. She offered encouragement as did Fr JJ O'Riordain, the Redemptorist, when he joined us to walk into Millstreet. Here at the bridge we crossed the Blackwater, dark and forbidding except for the torches that glowed on every side.

We dropped down from the wood. Night had fallen before we reached the Millstreet Road. A great crowd waited. Applause rippled as the Millstreet Pipe band fell into step. By now we had been joined by several hundred supporters. JJ O'Riordáin, of the great heart and the long step was reminding me that the great chief from the north, Red Hugh O'Donnell, had come this way and crossed the Blackwater on his way to Kinsale.

We were soon to reach 'the Boeing' a traditional ford across the Blackwater. That evening, we heard it before we saw it. It glowed and spumed fitfully between its darker recesses and those lit by cars. I wondered how O'Suilleabhain had managed here.

Our two boatmen sat quietly waiting. One told me that the crossing would take place with the help of a rope flung from the other side. We would grab hold of this and that would compensate for the strong 'drift'. Fr JJ said a prayer and we were on our way. The bank on the Duhallow side was lined three or four deep with people. It was silent. The rope was flung. Caught. Then a mighty cheer and we reached the bank. Willing hands pulled us up and ashore to be addressed by Donal O'Siochain and Tom Meaney.

We had crossed into the Barony of Duhallow in Cork to the wild hill country, dined with the O'Sullivan family and slept well that night. We had walked for 24 savage miles and had a great welcome for the people from the Irish Chiropody Association who came every evening to tend our poor feet. Clare Edwards from Killarney, the Kerry team physio, brought rest and calm to aching limbs. Each evening after the march, we broadcast that day's edition of *Donncha's Winter March* which soon caught the national imagination and helped many share in our mid-winter, eavesdropping on travel and travail.

The third day, was a matter of 40 stiff miles. We began at 7.30 in a torrent at the cross of Clonbannin where Tom Meaney launched us and Donal O'Siochain brought an almost bardic symbolism to our wet dawn. I will always remember John's Bridge beyond Newmarket. Raymond O'Sullivan reminded us of another savage encounter where the O'Sullivans put the attacking Barrys to flight, suffering the loss of four of their own party. Don Philip O'Sullivan Beara thus describes it:

> The ford was contested with red hot balls from both sides for about an hour. Four of the Irish fell, the Queen's men lost more and were forced to retreat ... There by the ford somewhere beyond Liscarroll, the dead were buried.

On a dark and windy evening we visited that place in the company of Dan Brennan and his wife, the landowners. Dan has always cherished this sacred place and its grove of trees.

Our welcome was warm but now it was dark, the wind whistling in our faces as we slogged on across country through Freemount and Dromina down a little used road towards Ballyhea. Michael McGrath was there: 'There are hundreds waiting in Ballyhea. You have twelve miles to go', he said.

There were, indeed, hundreds present. Jim Foley and the Charleville Brass Band played. Flaming torches filled the night. Ted O'Riordan, the great north Cork historian read to us an extract from '*O'Sullivan's Catholic History*, 'On a stormy night they pitched their camp in a desert place and vast solitude'. For us the stars glittered in a broad black sky in north Cork and John and Kathleen Leahy welcomed us to their place. Michael Byrne was among the shaking hands as was Paddy Collins who delivered a stirring welcome. It was the nearest I had been to home in a long time. The torches smoked and flamed against the darkness. So ended our longest day.

We are told that the O'Sullivans on the next day set upon the O'Dwyer clan for food and then halted near the village of Solohead, Co. Tipperary. On another march I would spend a night here in the company of the hospitable Collins family. We, too, halted there in the company of the

Archbishop of Cashel, Dr Clifford, who later joined us in Dundrum House where we were guests of Austin Crowe for that evening.

Osmonde Bennett arrived and by bed-time Sinead and I were fit for the rigours of another day. Rigours there truly were, for through rain, sleet and floods we set off to the Tipperary uplands, marching as best we could. Hollyford was first and on to Milestone where a car flashed its lights and a cheery voice shouted 'fáilte'. I discovered that Willie Corbett, well-known local historian, was the driver.

He was astounded when I told him that departure had been at 5.30 a.m. We turned for Upperchurch, which we reached for breakfast after some four and half hour's walking. The meal was provided by the local ladies and Pearse Duggan and Eamon de Stafort led the greeting party. It was now daylight and we set off once again to traverse the Sliabh Felim Mountains as rain poured down the mountain paths in yellow streams. We took a short break at the home of one of the ubiquitous Ryan clan. My throat muscles flexed and relaxed to a liquid welcome! It was a rough morning. I was heading for a live broadcast in the hall in Templederry.

Trees were planted as we prepared for the last march of the day into Latteragh in the barony of Ormonde. O'Suilleabhain Beara's little army was much diminished, cold and hungry by this time on their march. Don Philip wrote, 'He halted in the village of Latteragh, and threw his men into a rather small church and its enclosure. There was, in this village, a fort from which he was annoyed the whole night with firing and sallies from the garrison'. I slept in a house in a field close by where the church had been. I was in bed by 2.30 a.m.

We climbed an almost vertical hill the following morning and towards the summit I met Nancy Murphy, the historian. It was for once calm and peaceful quite unlike O'Sullivan's greeting as he went on his way. 'It was now the sixth of January, when at dawn a storm of red-hot balls blazed on O'Sullivan as he advanced'. My march, whatever else it was, was peaceful. The sun was rising pale pink in the wintry dawn, lighting the Devil's Bit away to our right. Knocksheegowna showed across the great valley of Ormonde.

We reached Cloughjordan around 1.00 p.m. to a welcome from Canon White and there, too, was Sergeant Michael McMahon who would be our guide and advisor across the Shannon. It's amazing how frost and night seem to fall together in the winter and this they certainly did under the romantic hill of Knocksheegowna. As we struggled towards that day's end I met Mary Cahalane whose kindness in planning and in helping to organise this great march are unforgettable.

Indeed, I dined with herself and her family in her lovely home and broke bread there after another brutal day. The summit of Knocksheegowna had been 'lit up' for the occasion and it was not difficult to imagine its importance in folklore as we went crunching by on the icy road. This very hill was celebrated as the other world seat of Una, 'fairy Queen' and guardian of the O'Carrolls of Ely. The hill, almost 1,000 feet high was once a place of Lughnasa celebrations on Garland Sunday.

Later that night we were guests of the late Michael Joe Egan from Castlebar who was now owner and loving carer of Redwood Castle, on the east bank of the Shannon, the ancestral home of the McEgans, scholars, bards and sometime sheriffs. He had renovated the old castle and we were his guests as was the late Canon Martin Ryan from Lorrha on that historic night. I thought quietly to myself that it was a far cry from the terrible place when O'Sullivan and what was left of his little force settled down for another night of fear in the boggy lea of this ancient castle. They had reached the Shannon and it had to be crossed.

They spent two days here 'building two ships of osiers and trees covered with the skins of twelve horses which they killed and whose flesh they all ate except for O'Suilleabháin, Diarmuid of Dursey and Diarmuid O h'Ulláchain'. The field has been known since as 'Poll na gCapall' and as I crossed it with Mr and Mrs Comber and a great throng from the Tipperary side the full horror of what took place there engulfed me.

We took some time off to attend Canon Martin Ryan's lovely and gentle Mass in Lorrha. Later on, Canon Martin said, 'history greets you every day. This is a place in which 'tis a privilege to live'. Indeed it was one of our great privileges to be there on a Sunday morning and to be hospitably greeted by the Canon and his housekeeper.

Michael O'Kennedy TD was not to be outdone and welcomed us to the land of the O'Kennedys and reminded us that they had been ever true to the course of Ireland and had never molested the Munster chief in 1603. As we were in Lorrha I couldn't but remember Tommy Reddan, a prince himself among Tipperary goalkeepers. Michael could not but heartily agree and cited Tommy as being among those who manned the goal before the 'untouchable syndrome was born'. Goalkeepers have since become what my friend Denis Conroy called, 'lads like the Mona Lisa, to be looked at but never touched'.

Our crossing of the great river Shannon took place on a misty morning with rime on grass and trees as the last Munster bonfire blazed near water's edge. The coracle on which I crossed was made by the pupils from the Vocational School in Kilcormac, Co. Offaly as a Leaving Cert Project.

It was almost circular, six feet in length by about four and a half feet in width. It consisted of hazel twigs bound together and covered with leather and impregnated with linseed oil. As I saw it for the first time, I remembered that of the two coracles made, the one made by Diarmuid of Dursey survived the crossing while the other, made by O'Malley for the Connachtmen, sank. The Connacht coracle was the same shape as mine. Too late now to call a halt. I said my goodbyes while Eileen O'Brien played a slow air and Canon Martin's housekeeper sprinkled holy water on us. I lay down in the tiny craft while the two oarsmen rowed strongly and bravely into the mist and the flood. One said quietly, 'twas a great rehearsal'. I nodded, wet-rumped but safe!

We were leaving Munster behind and with the memories of a bloody attack mounted on the Munstermen by Sheriff Donncha McEgan only to be repulsed with ferocity by the unseen galloglasses who remained hidden behind for such an eventuality. By the way the unwise Donncha lost his head.

My old friend Noel Treacy, TD and Sergeant Michael McMahon brought us in to dry land and a new phase in the Winter March. I had crossed at a place of history at the Ford of 'Ath na Coille Rua' about three miles upstream from Portumna Bridge on the ancient Pilgrim's Route to Ros Cré and on the scholar's path to the Bardic School at Ballymacegan. Only this time the natives were friendly!

That earlier O'Suilleabháin crossing had captured the imagination of many writers. Thomas Davis described it as 'The Great Romantic Achievement of the Age'. For me there is no doubt but that it was the highlight of the great march and there is no probability that I shall ever again cross the Shannon by coracle. I was exhilarated and frightened, being intertwined with our heroic past. Bishop Fogarty described the earlier achievement as 'O'Sullivan crossed the Shannon with the corpse of Ireland on his back'.

It was ten miles more to the sitting-room in Gortnamona in the home formerly owned by the Lynam family one of whom, Ned, was a friend and colleague of Percy French. They say that it was here that Percy wrote his great lament 'Gortnamona'. It was close to dusk when I went to the piano, the same one used by Percy French, and I played the chord of C and Patrick Conneally sang the song.

Joe Earley said 'six miles to Aughrim' and at this we were joined by another old friend Tom O'Sullivan who came all the way from Lahinch Co. Clare. It was a great gesture, quite typical of the man. Through the darkness, bonfires glowed mile after mile, little knots of people waved as we passed by. At one point, whole rows of candles glowed quietly from hedges on a still evening.

Aughrim was another cathartic moment for O Suilleabháin Beara and his reduced little army. Exhausted, quite worn out and perhaps disillusioned, they were suddenly faced by 'Henry Malby, an Englishman, Thomas Burke, brother of the Earl of Clanricarde with five companies of foot, two troops of horse and a band of natives'. The Malby party instantly attacked and what with the neighing of horses, the sheen on their armour, the braying of trumpets and the beat of their drums, O'Suilleabhain's advance guard were terrorised and unnerved. They broke in all directions and it is said that the Prince of Beara swiftly addressed the remainder saying:

> Since on this day our desperate fortunes have left us here without means or country, or wives or children to fight for, the struggle with our enemies before us now is for our bare lives: we have nothing else left that we can lose.
>
> In God's eternal name I ask you men, will you not rather fall gloriously in battle, avenging your blood than die like brute cattle in a cowardly flight? Our ancestors, surely, would never seek by flight to avoid an honourable death.
>
> Let us then follow in the footsteps of our sires: there is no other salvation. See around you that the country is now bare of woods or bogs; there is no concealment; the people of these parts offer us no aid. Roads and passes are blocked, even if we had strength to fly. Our only hope is in our own courage, and the strength of our own arms.
>
> Up then and attack this enemy, whom you excel in spirit, in courage, in achievements past, and holy faith!
>
> Remember that everywhere hitherto enemies who attacked us were routed by the Divine Mercy. Victory is the gift of God. Let us think then that Christ our Lord will be with his servants in their most dire need; and that 'tis for his name and holy faith that we are at issue with the heretics and those who cleave to them.
>
> Fear not this worthless mob: they are not men of such fame as we, nor used to fight as we are. When they see us heartily defy them, I do hope that they will turn tail, even as I look to it, that you will shew forth your courage and your faith.

The Munster men were roused and quickly faced the enemy and before long a fearful hand-to-hand engagement took place. O Suilleabháin was victorious, losing only 14 against the other army which scattered or ran in disorder. More than 100 were killed including their leader. O Suilleabháin took their colours, his men ate some of their horses and pressed on northwards.

As for me and my little force we entered Aughrim to great applause and went to Mass! Sinead, who never uttered a word of complaint asked for a loan of my scarf. She got it and of course, it was never returned! Fr Sean Slattery, an old and dear friend from Kiltormer, invited us to his new parish in Kilconnell and there we slept that sleep which is found nowhere else but after a great march.

Ahasgragh was home to Brid and Sean Ac'Donncha. It was here that Mattie McDonagh, the famous Galway footballer met us and marched on to Mount Mary. Snow and frost were more common as we journeyed on. Aodh de Blacam says that, 'snow was everywhere on Sullivan's march'. Before we swung left for Glinsk, I turned around to look back at a wintry scene. The cold and the early morning were almost mystical in their intensity. My thoughts were as much in the past now as in the present. I thought of all the nameless and quite forgotten men who always brought up the dangerous rear of Donal Cam's party. They were mercenaries, gallowglasses, brave unyielding fighting men.

> These in the days when heaven was falling
>
> The hours when earth's foundation fled
>
> Followed their mercenary calling
>
> And took their wages and are dead

The poet put it succinctly, 'what God abandoned, these defended'.

Six miles from Glinsk, an advance party came to meet us. Martin Ward, organiser and heart of his community, led horses, pipers, cars and children. A host followed. There were speeches and cheers of welcome at Glinsk Castle from which O'Suilleabhain had been turned fearfully away. Now all were welcome. A tree was planted. The children recited their poem for Donal Cam: 'This is not our promised land'. We had a medieval style banquet. Yes, indeed Glinsk was special.

Ballymoe was reached at dusk and like everywhere else we were received with pride. The local garda sergeant and his wife invited us into the Garda Station. This was the birthplace of Eamon Ceannt, piper and hero of 1916. Ballymoe was also birthplace of the famous Fr Flanagan of 'Boystown', portrayed in a Hollywood movie by Spenser Tracy.

On Sunday morning we left a silent Ballinlough just after 5.30 a.m. We felt the bitter lonely cold as, for once on our own we marched along the side of Sliabh O'Flynn and then down to Lake O'Flynn. Somewhere near here a bonfire blazed in a farmyard. I turned off the march for a flame-filled moment and shared the glow of the bonfire with the Carthy family, who may have been descendents of some of the marchers from Beara. This was another little pause to cherish and remember. We shook hands and said farewell. Daylight came below Fairymount. A snipe called out through the stillness. There was no talk. Sean Doherty TD arrived and cheered us up with talk and stories until we reached Frenchpark at around midday. After my broadcast, he brought me to a local christening party.

Day 13 began at the grave of Ireland's first President beyond Frenchpark. We had received a warm morning greeting from the children in the local national school. We began our day's recording at the grave and recited here a verse from Dubhghlas de hÍde. Paddy Ryan played a slow air on a cold morning fiddle as I recited:

> Guth na Gaoithe is na Taoide
>
> Ag siorthroid le cogadh cumhachtach:
>
> Muir tir, spéir, séideadh na gaoithe,
>
> Och! uile go léir is uaigneach

Frank Browne, storyteller and Larry O'Dowd, the piper joined us in a quiet recitation of 'An gleann 'nar togadh mé' by de hÍde. Our march was on. For one of the few mornings we were on our own as snowflakes swirled us on to Ballaghaderreen and the school band. There was welcome from Fr O'Doherty and later Bishop Thomas Flynn.

Monasteredan was our introduction to lovely Sligo where Master O'Gara, Fr Mulligan and the children welcomed us in their lovely school. We were joined by Madame McDermott and her staff. Proud of her ancestry she talked of the march to Kinsale and the attitudes of the local chiefs, McDermott and O'Rourke. 'They had no enemy', she said 'but the foreigner'. At the battle of the Curlews against Sir Conyers Clifford, 'They were men of no consequence and proved their worth'.

We were now entering a land of beauty and myth, driving towards the grey-faced Briclieve territory. The texture of the landscape reminded me of south Lebanon during my winter visit in 1978. The morning sun shone but was not warm. In the clear distance I could see Maeve's Knocknarea across the skyline from Ben Bulben and the Sligo drumlins. Nearer was the Hill of Kesh with its echoes of Diarmuid and Grainne. Colmcille and the battle of the books had his own place in this lunar landscape.

Joe Earley told us that the radio said that Ireland had seized up. It seemed that even the birds were freezing on the bare branches. We moved on slowly towards a tangled wood and by late afternoon we were entering our last great climb. My feet were cold and sore. I had a cold sore on my lip and thought of the story of O'Connor Kerry on the earlier march.

Red-eyed with the cold I read Don Philip's account. Poor O'Connor, probably the oldest man on the march addressed his feet which had quite given up. I knew the feeling. He said:

> Have you not gone through the most difficult trials these last three nights? Why do you now shrink from the toils of one night? Are not my head and the safety of my whole body more precious to you my most delicate feet? What doth it avail to have fled so far, if through your sloth we now fall into the hands of the enemy? I will assuredly make you shake off this sluggishness.

We are told that the old man jumped up and with great effort struck his feet against the ground, and squeezing out the matter, pus and blood he got up and began to march with the rest.

My musings were disturbed. I was called behind a rock and given an exuberant libation. The giver was the late Fr Pat Brady who talked as I drank. 'They got lost here and I'm not surprised,' he said. 'They had hallucinations or visions, call them what you will.'

I looked up towards the distant hilltop where Lloyd Praegar discovered the great Bronze Age cairn of Carrowkeel. We stood not far from this strange and wonderful place some 1,000 feet above sea level as Fr Pat pointed out to me some ravens flying from Kesh; the Ox Mountains and there in the distance was Croagh Patrick. This was the last conversation we ever had. 'This is a great thing', he said, 'but you know I feel for them, lost in time and place. Their past was gone forever and their future, well, doubtful'. He drove away into the afternoon sun and we carried on our way.

Later that night there would be Mass in Ballinafad with inspiring words from Bishop Dominic Conway. It was indeed in this very place that Don Philip tells us, 'a man clad in a linen garment, his feet bare, his temples bound with a white wreath .... an appearance well calculated to inspire awe'. He spoke to them and ultimately led them through the night. They groped on their way, feet slipping on loose stones, snow had heaped up in the wind as quite exhausted, the unhappy fugitives struggled on their way.

Our last day was cold. We walked an ancient pathway above Lough Arrow and often looked through the driving snow up towards yesterday's climbs. It was an emotional little party that left McDonagh's Pub to tramp the last seven miles into the vast desolation of Leitrim. The lake was snow-rimmed. A few swans sailed uncaringly by and a robin twittered song on a holly bush. Gerry Enright and the pupils of Carraigín Rua National School enchanted us. There was a great temptation to linger. Ted Berry said with truth, 'tis time to go lads, we have a place to go and a programme to make'.

Fr Dermod McCarthy, who had first mooted the idea, shook hands silently. We unveiled a plaque to Sinéad and myself at Knockvicar and crossed the Shannon for the second time. It was dark. A great moment before a blazing bonfire. St Patrick had crossed once near here. We were now all together on this black night. Those who went before us must have stirred to the pipes and the hundreds who marched along with us on our way to Leitrim village. Beth Earley handed me an Irish coffee. My hands were too frozen to hold it but not my throat to drink it. I have a last piece from the Chronicler: 'They reached Leitrim Fort about 11 o'clock, being then reduced to 35, of whom 18 were armed, 16 were sutlers and one was a woman ... I am astonished that Dermot O'Sullivan, my father, an old man near 70, and the woman of gentle sex were able to go through these toils'. They were all received 'with most honourable hospitality'. As indeed were we. Sinéad was the first woman since 1603 to complete the journey.

I was to make this epic journey on two other occasions since 1987, once for Earth Watch and most recently for 'Aid Link' and the Holy Ghost Fathers and the undomitable Fr Noel Murphy.

'This is journey's end for a space in the haven of O'Ruairc of Breffni and in the spirit of Donal Cam I bid you goodnight and goodbye. Slán Agaibh Go Foill.' – the last words uttered on the radio at the conclusion of 'Donncha's Winter March'.

Farewell And Fáilte

Now that I have passed my 65th birthday, it seems as if my working life has flown without as much as a pause. Since I was 15 years of age, work has been central to my life. Ambition and necessity have governed my needs. Most other personal concerns have been peripheral. Work and play coalesced. Time has always been groomed by the requirements of both.

My wife, Vera, has played a central part in guiding the family through many of life's inevitable storms. The children came in their time in orderly ranks. Feargal, the eldest was recently married to Dervilla, a splendid young woman from the Banner County, which fact I was recently reminded of, on my way to Croke Park to see Clare draw with Offaly. 'You're nearly one of our own ...' he said, reminding me of a new allegiance to the Blue and Gold! He has brought us much joy and fulfilment and is a young man of kindness, good humour and generosity, carrying with him many of the traits I most admire in people. Ruairi, who married Anne, a Dub, has more than a healthy slice of O Dulaing single-mindedness and good-humoured cynicism. He and Ann led the charge towards the brave young world of O Dulaing grandchildren. Both Cian and Aisling head the taskforce that leads to a certain form of immortality for all of us who have led and followed in the paths of our ancestors. Aisling, like her female forbears, is a lady of certainties while Cian's knowledge of motor-cars is quite extraordinary and will only be equalled by his good humour and need to play with computers. Donal, our third son, carried through his boyhood all the skills in hurling and football that I might have dreamt of and then carried into his young manhood many of the best traits of real Irishness. In his young wife Lorraine he has found his equal in love of the native language and country. The arrival of our newest grandchild, Caoilfhionn, like that of Cian and Aisling has privately electrified me. Donncha is the youngest who has gone to Donegal for love and fulfilment. Lorraine and he will find happiness and contentment in their own independence and unity. I'm sure he will one day grow out of wearing Dubs jerseys!

Donncha, who has recently joined the staff of Croke Park as administrator of their magnificent museum is, in many ways, pursuing my road into the past and people of the past. I was reminded of this the other day when researching for *Donncha's Highways Revisted*. I came across a quite extraordinary document written by a GAA committee in Doneraile to G. Levinge JP on 16 October, 1894. He was obviously a representative of Lord Doneraile in Doneraile Court. The letter, obviously a product of its time is both sad and startling:

Sir,

We intend playing a match (football) on Sunday next and would feel thankful if you would ask his Lordship for his permission to play in the deer park. We only want it for about an hour and a half and we promise faithfully that no damage will be done.

We will await a reply on tomorrow (Wednesday) evening at 6.30 p.m.

Yours respectfully,

F. Roche, J. O'Shea, J. Lillis, M O'Rourke.

What strides the GAA and indeed Ireland have made since then. I'm sure it will find a place among the memorabilia in Croke Park.

Sinead, I have kept until last. The only female, she has surprised and delighted me by joining RTE, becoming in the process, a typical RTE woman – which is, by the way a compliment! As the only female in the tribe she has never been over-burdened by her responsibilities or worn down by any of the male chauvinism that surrounded her. She brought new meanings to the O'Suilleabhain Beara March and was one of the reasons that the late Bryan MacMahon wrote us a wonderful letter on January 15th 1987.

'A Dhonncha, a chara na Páirte, Molaim tú féin agus arnó Sinéad go h-ard na spéire. Tá eacht deanta agaibh a mhairfidh i mBéaloideas ár dtíre. Las tú lochrann na staire ath-uair. Míle moladh aris. Bhí deora lem shúile nuair bhainis ceann cúrsa amach. Bhí imní orm go ndéanfa dearud ar O Conchuir Chiarraí nár dhéin! é féin is a chosa bhochta. Tóg bog anois é. 'That wonderful Winter March is o'er'. Ceap suaimhneas tamall. A bhuiochas leat. Maireann idealachas eadrainn go fóill.

I gcardas caoin Brian

My wife and family have well survived my ups and downs. They have all emerged more or less intact from a life that has often been less than fulfilling. The fact that the word 'survived' is used is entirely expressive of much. If there has been darkness, it is they who have lit the candles. I offer them thanks. Beidh laetheanta eile as na paoraigh. As I write here, it is 2.35 a.m. on a calm morning in August 1998 and I struggle against a vicious bout of coughing. The human condition confirms that time is passing.

Although my thoughts flow chaotically through the disparate years, I cannot say why President Nixon's visit to Ireland strikes me. Perhaps it's my own immortal words! 'The President has now stepped from the helicopter. He has his back to me and is smiling all over his face'. The desperation of filling commentary time! That was a lovely day down in Timahoe, Co. Laois when I very nearly didn't recognise the Artane Boys Band.

What about the long day in Ballyporeen in Co. Tipperary when, assisted by Mary Curtin, I described President and Nancy Reagan's visit to his ancestral hometown? This was a Sunday of trauma when the lady in charge of the FBI seemed intent on frustrating Gardai and RTE commentators on their duties. Still, apart from a memorable confrontation between our Ted Berry and the FBI, matters passed off easily enough.

One memory stands out. I arrived early on a quiet grey morning and was confronted by an officious member of American security. 'You gotta be frisked', he informed me. I did not wish for any such thing and a heated discussion took place. A friendly Garda Inspector heard me say, 'I will not be frisked by any foreigner in my own country'. Quick as a flash our Garda suggested a pleasant diversion. 'Maybe Donncha, you wouldn't mind being frisked by one of our own?' I would not, indeed, and when I saw her I was confirmed in my desire even to co-operate! Her touch was light and reassuring.

Great business was done in Ballyporeen on the day and on preceding days. It must be said, however, that when the Reagan wagons rolled on, interest slumped. Thus it was that my record, 'Reagan in Ballyporeen' never reached best-seller status! Neither its composer, Shay Healy nor its singer Donncha O Dulaing nor Con Donovan's shop window in Ballyporeen reaped any rewards. I thank Shay for writing a very funny pastiche of 'Donegan's Daughter'. K-Tel provided a splendid recording. Only the public miscalculated! As for me, well, I have hundreds of records to remind me of the time ....

> When Ronald he came from the States Himself and his Nancy were seen
> Paradin' the principal streets of beautiful Ballyporeen.

It was all great fun! I have been lucky enough to speak at the annual commemoration of Liam Lynch, the freedom fighter, at Kilcrumper, and I was to meet Con there again and again.

As I trawl through my memories, St Patrick's Day 1988 comes to mind. This was the day that I took part in the St Patrick's Day Dublin Millennium Parade – I led a group of worthies from Clontarf GAA Club to remind the nation that I would be marching from Inagh in Co. Clare to commemorate Brian Boru's famous march to Clontarf. We would march with great success for the Irish Wheelchair Association. But to come back to the St Patrick's Day Parade – I led our little contingent on a magnificent white horse named Carrigaline. Now, no longer young, he was beautiful and every inch a horse fit for a king. I was dressed as Brian Boru. Carrigaline was led by Morgan Llewellyn, the writer.

The parade across Dublin took several hours and much thanks are due to Colonel Billy Ringrose of the Army Equitation School who provided me with my steed. If there is a horsey heaven in the skies, Carrigaline must have an honoured place. He was a gentleman. It was another great experience and I won a beautiful Cuchulainn statuette splendidly inscribed 'Dublin Millennium St Patrick's Day Parade, 1988, I made the front page of *The Irish Times* in a fine photograph by Pat Langan. It's not often you see an image of a medieval King nervously using a mobile phone on horseback outside the Shelbourne Hotel. The phone belonged to Bill O'Donovan of RTE. The following morning I led my third Holy Land Walk. If I strode out like John Wayne for the next three or four days no one said anything! I just thought of Carrigaline's finely etched backbone.

The world of television brought me much excitement and not a little fame. My thanks go out to John Williams whose good humour and expertise led to the eccentric worlds of *Donncha's Travelling Roadshow, Donncha's Diary, Donncha's Adare* and *Donncha at Bantry House.*

John saw me as the 'country gent' complete with dickie bow, waistcoat and stetson. Wearing this unlikely attire I was introduced to a new world of viewers and listeners and thrived nervously on it. My long television interviews with the late Christy Ring were memorable and Dick Hill, then Controller of Programmes, saw fit to write me a congratulatory note. He was the only management figure ever to do this.

Our series from Adare Manor was magnificently crafted by John Williams and a crew whose skills were only equalled by their good humour and patience. The best performers in the land were among our guests and myself and my Irish wolfhound became national figures. Robert White, the great American lyric tenor, Bernadette Greevy, the Garda Band and many others graced the beautiful sets and my friend Thady Quin, the Earl of Dunraven, and his wife Geraldine mingled with guests and crew during the time that we can never forget.

Television work thrust me into the void of fame. It was a world far removed from radio. Everything took longer, the simplest interview, that I could have effected with speed and accuracy on radio, became a slow and tortuous affair where content was often subsumed under a mountain of extraneous but necessary effects. Lights, cameras, make-up, sound and people all pushed the subject into the background. The professionalism of the crews helped to soften the blow, but as a person accustomed to the simplicity, speed and immediacy of radio, I was the merest, tiniest cog on a vast and complicated television wheel.

I was concerned that my 'Highways People' and their 'stories' were pushed to the edges of the frame. Fear of a vast and technical unknown was often uppermost in my mind.

It was around this time, too, that I often acted as adjudicator for the 'Cailín Bán Festival' in Croom and an old schoolmate, the late Mossie Long officiated with Lady Dunraven Senior. One day she caught me somewhat surreptitiously surveying a well-turned female ankle and told me that I should always do this openly and honestly! I've never looked back!

The Travelling Roadshow was a visual image of the old *Highways and Byways* and brought us as far away as France on the Irish Ferries on a never-to-be-forgotten visit when the Hennessys of Killavallen introduced us all to the wonders of brandy. This was a night on which the wild geese had truly come home!

The world of County Cavan, courtesy of John Clancy of the Derrygarragh Inn introduced me to cures, skittles, ploughing, helicopters and a land where microphones were never heard. Indeed it was Fiach O'Broin who first brought me to a place where time lay dormant and generosity was endless.

Talking of generosity brings me to Tooraneena on the borders of Waterford and Tipperary. Tommy Hickey and his wife Kathleen, entertained me on many a long night of storytelling, singing and tales of superstition, folklore and the strange cure of Cahill's Blood. It was there we once re-created the story of Master McGrath, the weird world of 'Pettycoat Loose' and the thumb-smashing life of the Faction Fighters.

Indeed, Waterford and, in particular, the lovley town of Lismore has often been a beacon of fáilte. My thanks are more than due to the Dean of Lismore, the Cistercians in Mount Melleray and Mary Ryan and her family and many others in the gentle Déisc.

Television introduced me to the medieval world of Mardi Gras where John Williams, Margaret Costelloe and myself visited Venice for its unique but annual festival of excitements. I can clearly remember describing the scene to the viewers at home. There was no script, no prompts but all went fine until a moment came when several well-built and nubile young women deposited themselves before me. They were unclad and I could hear a Japanese commentator exclaiming his description in a state of high excitement. I had a problem. Something needed to be said. 'That's something we're seeing now', I said, 'that you wouldn't see most weekends around Buttevant!' True enough.

John Williams was responsible for creating a persona as physically near as possible to the subtle and complex world of *Highways and Byways*. I was concerned that the world of the imagination, as exemplified on radio might be lost in a visual sphere. Still, without the television we might have lost images of Jim Sweeney, the fairy man from Co. Longford who simply walked and talked his way into the homes of Ireland, unconcerned with effects or all the paraphernalia of a complex medium which took hours to do what radio did in minutes.

As I approached my 65th birthday, rumours of dire broadcasting times ahead of me spread like they always do in RTE. Truths, half-truths, most of them unpalatable concoctions whirled round me. I was more than somewhat led astray as some of those nearest to me affected knowledge of my future prospects, or lack of them. I, who had kept my cool over many years of trauma, was in danger of losing the run of myself. I finally did what I ought to have done long before then, set up an appointment with Helen Shaw, the new director of radio. She was kindness itself, and readily agreed to my continuing with *Fáilte Isteach* and suggested new avenues of work based on the vast archive of *Highways and Byways*, of which more later!

* * *

My initial introduction of the realm of *Fáilte Isteach* was not encouraging. Playing records on Saturday night was certainly not my idea of career opportunity. Still, I was constantly discovering that I was redundant in an area I had once practically invented. The blame lay not with my broadcasting colleagues but with others who hid behind the shadowy barricades of middle management in the Radio Centre. I was dropped a few less than tactful hints that I was no longer needed and that I was considered spent in radio terms. To those in the know and to those who felt they needed to know I was a spent force!

Bill O'Donovan became my facilitator-in-chief and encourager to a new and unlikely chapter in my broadcasting life. 'You should re-locate within the Radio centre,' he said. I did and was offered a desk, well, most of it anyway, and settled down in the world of Light Entertainment. Reactions, including my own, were muted, except, indeed from old colleagues in the Features area.

I was, or so I thought, surrounded by a polite and alien world. Pat Costello, the researcher broke the ice, 'You're very welcome Donncha', she said. I was invited to lunch and before long I became part of the world of Light Entertainment.

I began to surreptitiously investigate where I had never been before. Words like 'Comp-Op' (compere-operated) became meaningful. There was much gentle persuasion and one day I entered for the first time a 'Comp-Op' studio. This was so alien to my broadcasting life that I was scared and horrified. Mick McKeever kindly took me through a world so seemingly bizarre and unreachable as to make it at once possible and strangely achievable. Was this what I had to do to survive? Was this my new road as broadcaster? I spent hours on my own in studio. Disc after compact disc was played. The technical quality was quite astounding.

Another aspect of my new life would be 'live'. What most people did not know was that my broadcasting life had consisted of recordings. I had a few memories of the commentaries and very rare editions of *Highways and Byways* in a live format. I had never coped with sweaty palms and wildly beating heart. I was afraid. Age was in question. Still, go with the flow and on with the show.

The first night remains riveted to my mind. The dreaded compact disc machines sat loaded and waiting. The night's running order, including many of the listeners' favourites, was arranged. Most of the music I was quite unfamiliar with. Daniel O'Donnell, Foster and Allen, who had their first broadcast in *Highways and Byways* and others were all set.

Peter Browne clucked at my elbow. I cued myself into the national network and waited for my introduction from the Presentation Department. Peter said 'tis too late to go anywhere now. Good luck'. I know that he often felt that these preliminary moments were like the horses lined up at the Aintree Grand National. Then, I was on! Strange experience. My first time ever talking to listeners. No more communicating through the thoughts of a studio guest. Real, real radio. Record followed record, phone calls broke the rhythm. Extracts from letters all leading towards the end game before the pips before 11.00. Never, ever, crash the pips. Donncha's unlikely era with *Fáilte Isteach* had begun.

There was no turning back. But who was listening? Somebody unwisely, and in my hearing, described my time-slot as 'the sump of the night'. Time would tell. It did and quickly. The *Fáilte Isteach* listenership was loyal and almost instantly a new electricity was generated. Bill O'Donovan had read me well and as I turned the new pages I knew that whether for long or for short I had found my radio home.

The Saturday night foray into a world of high technology needed above all else, to express the simplicity of the medium. Satellites urgently speaking from dark night skies, worlds of digitalising material all hurtling towards a studio in Donnybrook from which Donncha reached out urgently and simply to those who wished to hear.

I needed, above all else, to feel that *Fáilte Isteach* was not just another well-oiled vehicle for new technology. It had to be the very opposite, be a broadcast where the same new technology provided a unique facility for radio broadcasts at their simplest and, if possible, at their best.

The programme at its simplest was of the chat and disc variety requiring the presenter to play the right disc at the right time. This was effected simply. Two compact disc machines were loaded and ready and a small coin was placed above that next for transmission and then moved on when the time came to play that disc. In that way the presenter always knew where he or she was. That was the theory. We were practically broadcaster-proof!

Fáilte Isteach needed a regular quiz, nothing fancy but enough to make people write. An Post kindly agreed to come in as sponsors and hardly a week goes by but we have upwards of 300 listeners not just entering the quiz but writing real letters. The 'Fáilte Family' is alive and well.

Peter Browne once had a tiny dog called Scooter and he has become the parent of the now fully grown *Fáilte* menagerie. They have lent a semblance of home and fun to the *Fáilte* world. Daisy, the cow, unchanged and unchanging is as warm and real as the dog and cat who sit by the fireside in our *Fáilte* Parlour of Dreams, sufficiently far away from Gandal the gander to feel safe. They all join with me and the listeners in the radio realities of our weekly meeting where memories of old times and dreams of the future commingle. What can one say of the listeners? They are those who listen every week, phone in most weeks and relish their part in the programme.

Aylesbury, Buckinghamshire was where I cut my 'waiting' teeth around forty years ago and now Bridie Bajal and others who remember those salad days have renewed contact and unlikely promises to meet again will be kept before the year is out.

Little Rock, capital of the State of Arkansas in the US is home to a nest of *Fáilte* Family members. We have once joined them at a birthday party and I am constantly reminded of a fantastic trek through Oklahoma, Arkansas and Mississippi when I led my walk for Afri to commemorate the long 'Choctaw Trail of Tears'. John and Mary Moore live in the Isle of Man and boldly state, 'not even wild dogs nor hissing ganders can drive us away from *Fáilte*'. Jim Cliggit who lives in Wales is clear: 'I'm at home every Saturday night' and from Walton Prison in Lancashire a prisoner has a clear message 'Several of the lads and myself listen in'. So, there is the far-flung homely world *Fáilte Isteach* and I thank Helen Shaw for kindly encouraging me to continue beyond 'that birthday' and to keep on 'pulling out the door after me'.

My life has changed. Certain freedoms have emerged. I belong now to the delicate world of the freelance broadcaster with *Fáilte Isteach* as my anchor and an amazing prospect once again of re-opening the secret world of Donncha's *Highways*. Only dream, only believe! My doctor tells me that long walks must reach into undiscovered bourns. The denizens of Saturday night's radio twilight zone are waiting – Brian Carthy and Brendan McKenna from Sport; Helen, Ciara, Jane, Carol and Kathy, the sometime tea-makers and pip-protectors of Presentation. Will Sandy and Maxi enter, clad as one should for a *Fáilte* evening of old-time waltzes and valetas.

The World of *Fáilte Isteach* has taken some giant steps towards the future. In the recent past I bought myself a computer and have now entered the mysterious regions of e-mail, internet, website and other such elements of my very brave and very new world. Listeners to *Fáilte Isteach* have not been slow to join me on my journey into the unknown.

George and Jean Middleton of Mexborough in Yorkshire 'feel that we are made welcome into the Parlour of Dreams every Saturday night'. Christine and Tommy Muir's e-mail came from North Ronaldsay and they were equally delighted, 'Isn't it great how e-mail brings us all into the parlour'. Mike Roger O'Sullivan of Bloomberg, New York remarked, 'I recently found out that I can listen to Radio Éireann live over the net at work in New York. Amazing. Fergal O'Donovan from Vancouver, Canada even told the time! 'Greetings from Vancouver, Canada, It's just gone 2.05 on a beautiful Saturday afternoon and we are enjoying listening to *Fáilte Isteach* over the internet'.

Michael Cannon, who lives in Villiers-Le-Bel in France entered our quiz and bade us farewell bilingually, 'Au revoir, slán agus beannacht; So our radio world grows large and small simultaneously.'

The Presentation Department has played a joyous and humorous role as next room neighbours and introducers to the Parlour of Dreams. Their introductions have helped to wind up the atmosphere and set the scene for many a great evening of *Fáilte* fun. Michael Cleere's heraldings have often come in poetic mode, drawing Donncha's chuckles even before the show has begun. Michael Comyn has become, not just one of the *Fáilte* family, but a rectifier of computer ailments and e-mail propagator among the denizens of the night and this is not to forget the role of Maxi and Sandy Harsch in wheedling a sometimes surprised and sometimes reluctant Donncha into the very late twentieth century. Apart from all this, the men and women of the Presentation Department have been known to make tea for guests in the Parlour of Dreams.

The warm world of *Fáilte Isteach* is now worldwide. I have come to recognise handwriting, style and postmarks. Many communicate every week by phone and by letter. How can I forget the likes of Mary Kershaw from Huddersfield, the likes of Patsy McCaughey from Trillick in Co. Tyrone, or Fr Pat Deighan, his housekeeper, Patricia and his friends including 'Frendees' the robin or Michael Moroney of the *Farmers Journal* who wrote a classic dissertation on a quiz question – the meaning of the word 'Gilt'. His letter told me that a gilt is 'a maiden female pig'. In case of any doubt, Michael quoted Professor Ian Moore who noted that 'maiden female pigs are called gilts' which describes 'the female virgin state of the pig'. It could only happen on *Fáilte Isteach*.

One could go on and on. Wonderful to say that listeners have become dear friends and sharers of all that is most fulfilling in my life. Early last year, when I was feeling unwell, I reluctantly paid a visit to a very kind and wonderful person, my doctor Bernadette Nolan. She was calmly startled by my somewhat raised blood pressure! I was scared witless and before long she had me installed in great comfort in the Mount Carmel Hospital in Dublin. I had every test known to man or woman! The consultant, the doctors, nurses and staff treated me with great kindness, managing to control my state of health and with the help of the good sisters, their friendship and their prayers, managed to steer my blood pressure back on an even keel. My days in Mount Carmel were especially memorable and the sisters and my doctor have become my friends.

Fáilte Isteach and my 'Parlour of Dreams' have brought much 'fun' to the world of radio. Indeed, what I call 'the arcane world' of Saturday night broadcasting has made an essentially cold medium warm, inviting and personal. It has made me feel part of the great broadcasters who have gone before me and through the 'new technology' of radio has catapulted 'old' Radio Eireann into this era of change, pursuing more than 70 years of Radio Eireann service down over wave after wave of progress into the darkest areas of cyberspace.

* * *

'That Birthday Party' was held in Studio 1 in the Radio Centre on a night when Donncha was 'enthroned' and Ronan Collins was on hand to ensure a safe and cheerful trip for the recipient of much love, affection, and good humour from all the wonderful colleagues. Truth, even in moments of high fun was not neglected. Ronan presented me with his own unblemished copy of my LP, 'Donncha Entertains'. He was not to know, of course, that I had 500 copies of same under my bed at home. Kathleen O'Connor, Micheál Holmes and Clare Byrne took care of all arrangements under the eye of Helen Shaw. An Taoiseach, Bertie Ahern wrote a kind letter in Irish, while Síle de Valera, our Minister was graciously present and I was reminded of the first time that I had met her at a tea party in her grandad's and granny's home in Áras an Uachtaráin. Bob Collins, the Director General, bore gifts of runners and a handsome cheque from all the friends, wrapped up elegantly and bilingually for the occasion. John Bowman was kind as was Judge Conor Maguire when he was not photographing all and sundry and he and Micheál Holmes played camera duets. The world of charity and walking was eloquently represented by Séamus Thompson of the Irish Wheelchair Association. Old friend and often travelling companion to America Senator Labhrás O Murchú carried Bertie's letter and a lot of memories with him and Kevin Hough spoke, as he always does, on behalf of the members of the now select band from 'Light Entertainment Radio'.

It could be truly said to have been a night to remember and made all the more joyous that it was not a wake in the truest sense. The remains was remaining!

Helen Shaw mentioned my archives, a vast collection of voices and events from my own past, a world encompassing the years from 1964 to the present. Would I be interested in having a look through them and presenting some of my favourites? Would I? The series was called *Donncha's Highways Revisited*, a series of nine half-hour programmes broadcast each Saturday morning during the months of July and August 1998. All the old friends have been a joy to meet again, a joy to re-discover and to discover in a tangible way how real and rich the series was and is!

A new generation of listeners has been introduced to the boyhood days of Eamon deValera. The 'women of the revolution', Nora Connolly O'Brien, James Connolly's daughter, Leslie, Bean de Barra, General Tom Barry's wife, Síle Grennan, among the last to leave the General Post Office in 1916 and others have helped to re-awaken memories and dreams I had once thought to be long-forgotten. Voices from my own childhood in Doneraile in Co. Cork have stolen back across the airwaves, among them the sardonic and humorous recollections of John B Keane's days of mixing 'scour specific' when he plied the chemist's trade in north Cork.

The story of the sinking of the *Lusitania* and the vivid memories of those who remembered it when they talked with me in the mid-sixties were as sharp as when I first heard them. We had, of course, the story of my 'Roman Adventures' prior to the Papal visit and the memorable and lovely voice of Canon Sydney McEwan. It brought a new generation back into time-past and transported that vivid past into the immediate present. So, we stride forward bravely and much-encouraged into the future.

1998 has certainly been a year for stepping into the sunlight of my new radio days. While it took some time to emerge from the chrysalis of a long broadcasting life, it also brought a new and surprising link with the land of my fathers in Kerry. My cousin Dennis came on a visit to Ireland from his home in United States. With one swift delivery he brought information that opened the door to the Dowling world in Glenmore, Camp in Co. Kerry. I discovered that my grandfather, Denis Dowling, had married my grandmother, Julia Walsh, on 22 February 1868. My own father Daniel was born in 1896 and certificates assiduously sought out bore accurate witness to the lives of my aunts and uncles.

Closest of all, however, to the lives of the Dowlings were a series of letters from Kerry to members of the family in USA. My grandmother Julia was the most diligent chronicler of her time. The first letter, however was written by my aunt to her brother in America on 19 October 1914. It contains a graphic account of my grandfather's death:

> I had him laid out at 4 o'clock Wednesday.
>
> We had everything prepared beforehand. We had the iron bed in the kitchen all draped in white.

She returns to the moment of his death:

> On Tuesday night a change came ... I recited the prayers for the dying ... we know for certain that his end was drawing nigh ... it's the saddest parting and he certainly ... a happy place in heaven ... which he so dearly sought.

A letter to my Uncle Pat in America tells how he 'remained conscious up till the last moments even called Danny (my father) to his bedside and was speaking to him on business and what they should do that day.' She concludes simply, 'our home is very lonely now'. My grandfather died on 15 October 1914, aged 75 years.

Grandmother Julia's letters written in a clear hand, are full of practicalities as when she writes in September 1920: 'I feel glad to think that ye can have fresh eggs from your own fowl house.' The world of west Kerry transmitted to America!

In December 1921 she reflects on the national situation:

> We got happy tidings today when our people came from Mass, they told me that the priest had preached that peace was granted. It was a happy news for everybody, especially for mothers.

By 19 July, 1922, she was less hopeful than before and wrote of 'nothing gained but war and trouble, sure poor old Ireland is in an awful state.' She had better news of my father by 1924:

> I suppose you heard that Danny is in the Civic guards in Ballycotton (Co. Cork). He writes to me every two weeks. I felt awful lonesome after him, though knowing that he stayed too long around here, the creature, when I would be sick or anything wrong with me, he used to be kind and good to me, staying in my room as company for part of the night. He says that he is well and in a nice place near the chapel where he can go to Mass every morning.

She concludes her praise of my father with a typical mother's fears for her youngest: 'There must be danger in those places with robbing and plundering although he does not complain of those matters.' I must say that her letters make me prouder than ever of my father and my own childhood memories confirm much of what she wrote about him, in particular, the facts of his daily attendance at morning Mass in Doneraile and in Charleville.

These letters, and many more, so lovingly kept by my cousin Rita in America have brought me closer than ever before to those who came before me and I am glad to pass them on to those who come after. Kerry is closer than ever before. In this way the Dowling history continues and Grandmother Julia deserves all my thanks and remembrance. No wonder my father continued to write and send her 'plugs' of tobacco. Ar dheis Dé go raibh a hanam.

* * *

As I come towards the end of this book, the year has turned and autumn has succeeded a wet and listless summer. It is 4.50 a.m. on a miserable morning in August 1998 as I strive to reach conclusions. Writing a book about myself sometimes seems an arrogant sort of business and when it coincides with later middle-age and the onset of old age it seems like what we in our business call 'a wrap'.

But, that is not the case. Health seems at least adequate if not, indeed, very well and new broadcasting projects are beckoning and, by the time this tome is published, I shall have undertaken at least one long walk. Lest I have forgotten to say it, these walks have filled my life with happiness.

Recently I had the pleasure of attending an Irish Vintage and Tractor rally in Ballyroan in Co. Laois. Many reminded me of an earlier visit to that friendly place perhaps a quarter of a century ago and now a new generation, just as kind, just as generous, just as welcoming awaited me. My walking and broadcasting world awaits me.

There are new adventures ahead, new hills to climb, goals to achieve and life to live. As they, whoever they may be, say 'places to go and people to meet'. It's quite simply time to move on. The internet awaits. My 'inbox' is full and the 'outbox' needs replenishing. Time, as I said, is positively marching forward.

Before, however, I lay down my pen, I humbly thank all who have made this 'life' a fact. EM Forster, in writing his 'Aspects of the Novel', suggested death is the best terminator for characters, but I am not a 'character'. The day is quietly and silently dawning, the echoes of my past gently 'fade into grey' never, yet, 'into black'. My pen is laid aside for the present. Publication will be a great new adventure. Beidh lá eile ag an Paorach and with the way progress is being made in the north, there will be a new day, too, for 'Cáit Ní Dhuibhir.'

As for me, I'll take my own advice and pull out the door after me. May the road rise to us! Slán agaibh go fóill.